Trailersteading

Trailersteading

*How to Find, Buy, Retrofit, and Live Large
in a Mobile Home*

Anna Hess

Skyhorse Publishing

Skyhorse Publishing books may be purchased in bulk at special discounts
for sales promotion, corporate gifts, fund-raising, or educational purposes.
Special editions can also be created to specifications. For details, contact
the Special Sales Department, Skyhorse Publishing, 307 West 36th Street,
11th Floor, New York, NY 10018 or info@skyhorsepublishing.com.

Skyhorse® and Skyhorse Publishing® are registered trademarks of
Skyhorse Publishing, Inc.®, a Delaware corporation.

Visit our website at www.skyhorsepublishing.com.

10 9 8 7 6 5 4 3 2 1

Library of Congress Cataloging-in-Publication Data is available on file.

Cover design by Erin Seaward-Hiatt
Cover photo credit Anna Hess

Print ISBN: 978-1-63450-410-2

Printed in China

Table of Contents

Trailersteading

Preface

Our trailer is slowly but surely becoming an integral part of our permaculture homestead.

When I originally put fingers to keyboard to begin writing my indie-published edition of *Trailersteading* over two years ago, I have to admit that the idea began as a bit of a joke. Nearly every homesteader I saw profiled in magazines, books, and blogs was either living in an artisanal house—straw bale, cob, log, etc.—or was saving and planning in order to build the same. And here I was enjoying my time in a single-wide trailer that had more years on it than I did and that my husband had found free for the hauling. The contrast made me laugh . . . and also made me want to tell the world about my own adventure.

Still, when the time came to self-publish the ebook (because what respectable publisher would even consider such a title?), my hand hovered over the mouse pad with trepidation. Could I handle the inevitable outcry from readers who had bought into the American dream of home ownership and felt threatened by my countercultural housing choices? I fully expected reviews like this one, which appeared on Amazon not long after publication:

"As someone who works full time to pay a mortgage and have health insurance and save for retirement and provide a stable future for my family, and to just generally live like a civilized human being, I was struck by how many of the people featured in the book tried to act as if being lazy and irresponsible is a noble feature . . . Would love to see if they can sustain that lifestyle forever (without being a burden on us taxpayers)."

Yes, my book had clearly struck a nerve, just as expected.

What I didn't expect was the hundreds of five-star reviews from homesteaders who were itching for a less expensive and time-consuming alternative to the traditional path of home ownership. Readers called the book "new and exciting," "a groundbreaking literary effort," and "very informative," and several mentioned that *Trailersteading* had inspired them to retire early by embracing life within an old mobile home. The ebook was snapped up by thousands of readers within its first months of life. I began to see the term "trailersteading" bandied about on the Internet outside the context of my book, and, to my surprise, a publisher thought perhaps a traditionally published edition of the title made sense after all.

So why begin this second edition by reprinting such a scathing review? As I mulled over the concept of trailersteading, I realized that the largest impediment standing between many of us and true freedom is concern about what our friends and family will think of our life choices. Will your mother-in-law be scandalized when you downgrade from a mortgaged McMansion to join the ranks of the permaculture trailer trash? Will you stop being invited to all the right parties when you show up with mud on your boots and callouses on your fingertips? The review above should help you prepare for the worst, but I wouldn't be at all surprised if far more of your peers are intrigued by your lifestyle choices than condemn them. In the end, you'll likely discover, as we did, that most people are too busy with the minutiae of their own lives to care what you do or where you live.

So the decision really comes down to what works for your own family. And there, the scales tip strongly toward trailersteading. By choosing to homestead in a trailer, you can net more time to share with loved ones, more energy to spend on hobbies and passions you enjoy, and more money to save for retirement. You can reach your goals faster, and you may find, as we have, that every year of your trailersteading adventure is better than the last. So come join the ranks of homesteaders who have chosen to embrace voluntary simplicity in a mobile home, and you too can rake in the rewards of this off-beat lifestyle.

Introduction

Why live in a trailer?

Our trailer in fall 2012.

"You should write about your biggest successes and failures as a homesteader," my father suggested during a recent phone call. At the time, my husband Mark and I had spent the last six years learning to grow our own food and to make a living without a boss, but I had to smile because I knew the item at the top of my success list was also at the top of my father's failure list. Rather than building a beautiful house that could grace the pages of *Mother Earth News*, Mark and I opted to lower our housing costs to nearly $0 by living in a free mobile home.

The average American family spends 20 percent of their income on housing, with the median price tag for rent or mortgage being over $16,000 per year. And many homesteaders-to-be go so far into debt building or buying their home that they're forced to put off their self-sufficiency goals until after retirement. Even folks who opt to build a "tiny house" (more on this term in the next chapter) generally spend years of their time on the project and end up with an albatross of a mortgage slung around their necks.

Minimizing your housing expenses can be a way of paying off debt or saving for a large purchase.

But there *are* cheaper housing options. A friend wanted to pay off his credit card debt, so he moved out of his apartment and lived in his car for a few months. My brother resided in a converted chicken coop for years. And a visitor to my childhood farm simply pitched a tent in each new location that he passed through.

Overview of the initial startup costs and annual energy bills of the full-time trailer-dwellers profiled in this book.

	Square feet	Purchase price	Installation price	Initial renovations	Annual energy bills
Anna & Mark, "Our mobile home adventures"	500	$0	$2,000	$500	$1,017
Wendy & Mikey, "Cheap and green"	1,200	$1,000[a]	$0	$11,086	$415
Jonathan & Andrea, "Trailer park to woodland paradise"	924	$8,000	$12,000	$610	$2,049
Sara & Seth, "Starter home for a young family"	960	$15,000	$7,000	$0	$840
David & Mary, "An incognito trailer"	840	$15,773[b]	$884[b]	$0	$1,690
Brian and Stepha-nie, "Remodeling their way into debt-free home ownership"	975	$14,500[c]	$0	$750	$1,560
Lindsey & Keith, "A crazy, cobbled-together, split-level mobile home"	1,680	$7,500[d]	$3,000	$9,500	$1,950
Harry & Zoe, "Early retirement in a trailer"	1,568	$52,000[e]	$0	$0	$2,100
Jimmy & Alice, "A holler full of family"	1,480	$55,000[f]	$0	$0	$2,300

[a] Trailer already in place on land, so I used the value estimated by the insurance company.
[b] Adjusted for inflation to show equivalent 2014 dollars.
[c] Includes 0.28 acres of land, a well, septic system, electricity, concrete driveway, carport, and screened patio.
[d] The first trailer came with the land and isn't included in these figures.
[e] Assessed price of mobile home on a masonry foundation, with utility connections and an installed heat pump.
[f] Adjusted for inflation to show equivalent 2014 dollars. Purchase price included half an acre of land.

The truth is that simple housing doesn't have to be so extreme. Used mobile homes are a very low-cost housing option that allow you to improve your living situation a bit at a time when you have the cash, but social stigma keeps many homesteaders from even considering the trailer option. And yet, if a trailer allows you to live without debt, to keep your ecological footprint to a minimum with energy bills at or below the national average, and even to blend right in with traditional house-dwellers after a few years, why not go for it?

Case study: Our mobile home adventures

I dreamed of homesteading ever since my own back-to-the-land-dreaming parents threw in the towel and moved our family to town when I was in the third grade. And I have to admit that none of my fantasies included a trailer. I researched straw-bale houses, earthships, and cob. I drew floor plans and crunched the numbers on passive-solar heating.

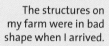
The structures on my farm were in bad shape when I arrived.

Meanwhile, I was saving my pennies to purchase as much land as possible. I ended up with 58 acres of swamp and hillside (and a couple of arable corners) in southwest Virginia, including a barn with huge holes in the roof and a hundred-year-old house that was falling down. In retrospect, I should have fixed up that house, dilapidated as it appeared at the time, but I had very little experience with building and my father deemed the structure unsafe. So down it came.

A year after buying my dream homestead, it was looking less and less like I'd ever live there. The farm had only cost $600 per acre and I'd gotten most of that money as a no-interest loan from a friend, but I was still in debt and had very shallow pockets. Using a very low-ball figure of $20 per square foot for a traditional stick-built house (meaning that it would be framed with lumber like two-by-fours), a twenty-foot-by-twenty-foot house would cost $8,000 to put together, plus months of labor. Was my dream going to wash out without even a trial run?

As my hopes reached their lowest ebb, my husband-to-be, Mark, marched into my life. I had been raised by parents who adamantly denied their hippiedom, but who still managed to raise three children below the poverty line while giving us a very middle-class education—voluntary simplicity in action. Mark's parents, on the other hand, had pulled themselves up by their bootstraps, ensuring that they could provide new clothes and a nice house for their kids. But Mark's family heritage lay in hard-scrabble farming in eastern Kentucky and trailers were part of his culture. In fact, his own mother had spent several years of her life in a mobile home (albeit the most beautiful one I've ever walked through), so Mark's mind was wide open to housing possibilities.

"Do you really want to get a full-time job just to pay for building a house?" Mark asked. By this time, he was a member of my homesteading team and was quickly wiggling his way into my heart. I had lived in a tent for a year and found the experience presented little hardship, so it wasn't that I thought a trailer was beneath me. Honestly, I simply hadn't considered the option. But once Mark raised the question, I was quickly swayed by the idea

Our windowless trailer in its original mobile-home park.

of having a ready-made living situation that would let us move to the land right away and put our energy into creating a vibrant vegetable garden—even then, I cared much more about apple trees than about interior design.

Our initial search for a trailer took us far afield. We hunted through classified ads, looking at trailers in the $1,000 to $2,000 range. The world was astonishingly full of trailers for sale—big ones, small ones, trailers reeking of cat piss, and fresh new trailers that seemed as fancy as any home I'd ever lived in.

Then reality struck. The price of the trailer wasn't the primary consideration—location was. We were going to have to hire a trailer-hauling company to transport our mobile home to my farm, and those companies charge by the mile. So the closer a find was to our land, the better. We stopped reading classified ads and started rolling down back roads near our farm. Within hours, we stumbled across a trailer park fifteen minutes away and asked its proprietor if he had a mobile home he was willing to sell for $2,000 or less.

"You can have that one over there for free," he said, pointing to a 1960s model, windowless and empty at the edge of the park. "That is, if you haul it off." And that's how we found our new home.

We were lucky that our free trailer was small—10 feet wide by 50 feet long. In fact, when we got the trailer-hauling crew to come look at our property, they said that a larger trailer would have been impossible to pull

A bulldozer allows a trained crew to move trailers into the most surprising locations.

into our house site. Even in preparation for our tiny trailer, the crew told us to cut big openings in the forest at each curve in the driveway to give the vehicles room to maneuver. After that, we had to wait and wait and wait until the driest day of the year when a bulldozer wouldn't get stuck in our muddy floodplain.

My father was never keen on the idea of his daughter living in a trailer, and although I've happily ignored most of his parental admonishments, I wish I'd followed the advice to absent myself from the farm on moving day. At a rate of hundreds of dollars per hour, I could see my small collection of backup cash slipping away with every hang-up. As I watched our crew jack the trailer up so that it could roll across the creek, my heart was in my throat, and I gulped as a low-hanging branch ripped a hole through the trailer's tin wall. But, finally, the bulldozer yanked our new/old trailer into the spot that we'd cleared for it amid two acres of blackberry brambles. They even carefully aligned the trailer with the long sides facing north and south for passive-solar gain. Home!

We closed in our trailer with double-glazed windows.

Over the next few months, Mark filled the gaping holes in the trailer's walls with double-glazed windows, which we'd gotten free or cheap over the last couple of years in preparation for our eventual home. We ripped up ancient carpets to reveal not-too-bad linoleum, hauled out a broken washer and dryer, and mended a few leaks in the roof. Overall, I'd say we put maybe $2,500 into installing and closing in our 500-square-foot home—$5 per square foot—and the vast majority of that went to the trailer-hauling company for their impressive feat of moving our mobile home onto our remote property.

Over time, our trailer gave us freedom to focus on our dreams, so Mark was able to scratch his inventing itch and come up with an automatic chicken waterer (www.AvianAquaMiser.com) that began to put bread on the table. I was able to spend my days doing what I loved as well—playing in the garden and writing about my adventures. As other trailer-dwellers will remark in the case studies later in this book, we enjoyed the camping elements of early trailer life, and valued the way it made us take part in the natural world.

Nature sometimes comes to visit us in our trailer.

Although the construction of trailers is somewhat shoddy, that very simplicity gives the homeowner freedom to try his untrained hand at home improvement with impunity. I learned about studs, insulation, and electric wiring, while Mark completely changed the layout of the main room, ripping out a divider to combine the kitchen and living room into one large space. I would have been afraid to make such major changes in a traditional house, but working on our trailer was a bit like playing with Legos—we couldn't go wrong.

Keeping our housing simple allowed us to work only part-time and to spend the rest of our hours experimenting and gardening. Here, Sussex chickens explore our oilseed radish cover crop in fall 2011.

Doing what you love often requires you to tighten your belt at first, but then money seems to move toward you via osmosis. Without spending much time on the money-making side of our operation, our income increased to the point that we were able to start thinking about improving our living quarters without going into debt. As I'll explain in later chapters, we added an alcove so we could install an energy-efficient wood stove and hired a friend to put on a roof and a couple of porches. Other trailer-dwellers have aimed their home-improvement funds at insulation and interior design, with the result that many visitors can't even tell they're walking through a mobile home.

The best part about our trailer is purely financial. After our initial startup costs, we can now live on next to nothing. While most folks around us are paying rent or a mortgage, our housing bill comes down to a measly $300 per year that we throw at the county in property taxes, and we have no debt to force us into an off-farm job.

Me, Mark, and Lucy at home.

I consider the trailer one of Mark's biggest strokes of genius because it has allowed us to work only a few hours per week on income-driven projects. After that, we can spend the rest of our waking hours pouring our hearts and souls into becoming more self-sufficient.

If you subscribe to voluntary simplicity, you could do much worse than following Mark's advice and scouring the countryside for a free trailer to live in. Just make sure you have plenty of other passions to fill up the time you would have spent pinching pennies to pay for your mortgage with a full-time job.

What is a mobile home?

Before I go any further into my ode to the trailer, I should back up and make sure you know what I'm talking about. The term "trailer" is a reminder of the roots of the mobile home, in the small travel trailers many people haul behind their primary vehicle while vacationing. Beginning in the 1950s, these travel trailers started to be marketed as a cheap housing option, at which point they were enlarged and renamed "mobile homes."

Mobile homes are distinguished from modular homes by the wheels and axles underneath the former. While both mobile homes and modular homes are constructed in a factory, modular homes are brought to their new location on a flatbed truck, hauled atop a foundation with a crane, and never moved again. In contrast, mobile homes can be pulled behind a large truck and moved multiple times, and they are generally taxed and legislated as vehicles rather than as real estate. The implications of your home being a vehicle are that your property taxes will usually be lower and you won't have to jump through as many building-code-related hoops before moving in; on the negative side, a mobile home also tends to depreciate in value like a car rather than appreciating like a house, and many banks have fewer financing options available for mobile homes.

Within the category of mobile homes, you can choose between single-wide and double-wide models. The latter is made by combining two single-wides that each lack a wall on one side, so you end up with a larger living space (twenty feet or more in width). However, double-wides are very difficult to move after their initial installation and they tend to hold their value like a traditional home, so chances are the free or cheap used trailers you'll come across will be single-wides.

Case study: Cheap and green
Choosing to live in a trailer

"The low cost of our trailer allowed us to create a home with money in our savings," said Wendy. "A different building option would have required a mortgage."

"I was the creative director in a marketing firm in New York City before moving to Truth or Consequences, New Mexico, to build a homestead made of waste with my partner Mikey Sklar," Wendy Jehanara Tremayne said. "All the projects that I do explore a single question, 'Can one live an uncommodified life?'"

Wendy and Mikey make a living with various online enterprises, including selling wildcrafted and homegrown herbs. You can see their handmade products at store. holyscraphotsprings. com.

"We had been living in a small house but wanted something a little less traditional," her partner Mikey explained. "When we noticed an RV park for sale, we jumped to buy it. The trailer on site had been left behind."

"The trailer on the land we bought was a modified single-wide from 1967 and had several additions that enlarged it to 1,200 square feet," Mikey said. "It wasn't pretty. Brown paneling and shag carpet covered most of it, even some of the ceiling."

Photo credit: Wendy Jehanara Tremayne and Mikey Sklar

"At first we did not know we were going to live in it," Wendy said. "We considered hauling it to the landfill. It was old and crappy. The insurance company valued the jalopy at $1,000. The cost to haul it to the landfill was estimated at $5,000. New building came at the cost of $200 per square foot. We determined that for $10 a square foot (less than $10,000) we could remodel it, and so we did."

"The remodel amounted to sheetrocking the walls, installing bamboo floors, and we repurposed throwaway wood that we found in a dumpster into trim for the windows. We tiled the bathroom floor and counter with second-hand chipped tile that we laid in a mosaic pattern," Wendy said. "We added a coat of paint to the exterior, re-skirted with inexpensive flashing, and trimmed it in dumpster-dived wood that we resurfaced."

Photo credit: Wendy Jehanara Tremayne and Mikey Sklar

"Our trailer park was expensive, so the move was not about saving money," said Mikey. "Remodeling the old trailer saved us the headache of trying to build a house from the ground up in a remote area where there are limited resources."

Photo credit: Wendy Jehanara Tremayne and Mikey Sklar

Wendy and Mikey furnished their home largely with found materials and a lot of elbow grease.

"We also had taken a pledge to live out of the waste stream, thus the name of our blog Holy Scrap," said Wendy. "Remodeling [the trailer] was the greenest choice; it prevented the whole place from becoming landfill."

Mikey added, "We have a saying: 'The greenest house is the one that is already there.' We didn't like the idea of hauling a perfectly usable living space to the dump in order to avoid the stigma of living in a trailer. Insulation and thermal mass reduce home utilities. They are not standard issue in trailers. But we have found that utilities can be reduced by adapting to the environment. In the winter we wear a sweater and in the summer we wear shorts."

"Because our trailer was valueless (according to the insurance company, who said it was worth $1,000), it presented us with a risk-free starting point and an opportunity to learn new skills," Wendy said. "The renovation taught us to use tools and work with building materials. Though the trailer may not last forever, the skills will!"

"We had never renovated anything before," added Mikey. "Working on an old and valueless trailer presented little risk. It was easy to find the courage to try new things."

Debt-free housing

A shaded outdoor space makes summer in a trailer much more enjoyable.

Photo credit: Wendy Jehanara Tremayne and Mikey Sklar

Wendy has a less-than-mainstream approach to debt and the American dream. "When I see people driving new cars and living in new houses, I wonder if they do so because they did not have the money to make another choice. Did they have to get a sucker's car loan or mortgage with bad terms because they had no liquidity? I wonder about what it might be like to live a debt-heavy life that requires working a lot to support debt.

"Poverty looks different today. A debt-free life in a trailer means freedom. Fancy new cars and homes are symbols of a trade-off.

"Our trailer is in a part of the country in which trailer life is common. It's not like New York City. In New Mexico, trailers are not associated with poverty. Where we live in Truth or Consequences, many people buy old trailers and fix them up in the same way that we did, new sheetrock and wood floors. The weather is mild in New Mexico, the climate dry; trailers last."

"I don't think living in a trailer will make you popular, but it doesn't seem to hurt," interjected Mikey. "Our town likes them. It's cool to own one. We have a micro-scene of people who live in remodeled trailers."

"Living here changed my perception of poverty and abundance," Wendy added. "When the stock market crashed in 2008 and foreclosures hit

14 percent in nearby cities, the community we live in, largely made up of trailers, had a foreclosure rate of less than 4 percent. At first I couldn't understand this. New Mexico is a poor state and Truth or Consequences is a poor city even by New Mexico standards. This is a modern shift in what poverty looks like. People in wealthier areas living in more expensive homes were losing them to banks while poor people in southern New Mexico were living life as usual. People lived in inexpensive trailers that had long been paid off. Life went on as usual. We hardly felt a blip. Likewise the thrift shops and consignment stores on Main Street and Broadway stayed open. They continued to sell used stuff. New Mexico was so good at being poor that, when the economy collapsed, we didn't notice."

Disadvantages of the trailer life

Although both members of the couple were enthusiastic about many aspects of trailer life, when asked if they would take a hypothetical debt-free "dream home," Wendy and Mikey expressed willingness to upgrade. "We're growing out of our trailer," Wendy said, mentioning two shipping containers they have in the yard to supplement their 1,200-square-foot trailer and additions. "We're considering buying two more [shipping containers] so that we have dedicated space for fermenting and for our cottage industry."

Photo credit: Wendy Jehanara Tremayne and Mikey Sklar

One shipping container houses Mikey's electronics lab and another provides storage space.

When it came to the dream home, Wendy had lots of questions. "I wouldn't wish to take on the taxes, utilities, or maintenance of such a place. I am sure I would not want to clean it! But we could use the space for a workshop, bigger and higher functioning kitchen, and our cottage industry. My answer really hinges on the details. What is that home made out of? What is its orientation? Does it face south? How is it heated and cooled? If it were a smart home, built sustainably, windows facing south, and space laid out well, I might say yes! Since the deal includes that I couldn't sell it, it would have to come ready to go and not require an investment of my labor or time."

Mikey's reaction was simpler: "Yeah, I'd take it," he said, "assuming the home was in an area I wanted to live. Trailers are okay, but I'd rather have a real house."

Painting the seams of the roof with an elastomeric paint prevents leaks during New Mexico's sporadic rains. Since the trailer cost so little, the couple have been able to move off the grid with solar panels. They do spend a small amount of money per year in connection fees to the electric and gas grids as a backup.

Both Wendy and Mikey recognized major downsides to their trailer life. Wendy wished the structure had a better roof, recognized that the fiberboard drop ceiling can bear no weight, and wasn't thrilled by the loud forced air. Mikey added leaks at the junctions between trailer and additions, inexpensive fixtures, and an orientation wrong for passive-solar gain to the list of disappointments, along with low ceilings that threaten to bump the heads of tall visitors. Finally, both were less than thrilled with what Wendy calls "barely working single-pane windows," but they've chosen not to replace them because, as Mikey explained, "The resale value is questionable."

Photo credit: Wendy Jehanara Tremayne and Mikey Sklar

Wendy leverages the trailer's windows for herb-drying.

"If I didn't live in a trailer I'd put a wood-burning stove in my living room," added Wendy. "Instead I have the less-than-wonderful wall-mount gas heater."

A parent's perspective

Since social stigma is one of the reasons many homesteaders choose to steer clear of trailers, I was interested to hear from people near and dear to our trailersteaders' hearts. Mikey's mother and father agreed to share their impressions with me, and both were very supportive of the couple's decision. They seemed more floored by Mikey's choice to quit a job that had provided a $110,000 Christmas bonus than by his current lifestyle.

"What did surprise us was Mikey's and Wendy's return to barter-economy basics, self-help carpentry, and construction skills," reported David, Mikey's father. "When they first got [to New Mexico], Mikey used to trade fresh bread for information. Equally, everything had to be natural in origin or recycled.

"Over the years, they found new ways to make money. Used local produce to make tea, wine, beer, and bread. They remain young at heart, joyfully together, and enjoy a freedom of time and lifestyle they never could have maintained in the structured environment of the city or their jobs. They raft on inner tubes down the Rio Grande, and eat their own fruit and vegetables.

"Are they happy? Their lifestyle is rewarding and changes as much as they do. Wendy writes and makes new discoveries every day in yard and kitchen.

Mikey invents and explores new things from sales on eBay to 12-day wine-making. They are exciting to talk to, and involved in their quest and each other. No parent can ask for more."

Wendy's and Mikey's recommendations

Mikey's advice for folks considering trailer life is simple: "Remodel right away and be sure you have somewhere else to live while doing it. For a trailer to be super-cool, it needs to be clean. Ditch the shag and hide the paneling."

Wendy and Mikey share their home with two cats and a dog.

"I recommend trailer living provided you live in a mild climate," Wendy said. "I certainly recommend remodeling trailers of any size and using them for a home, guest house, or artist workshop. Small trailers make wonderful projects for learning new skills. They are not expensive to remodel and can often be done using waste found free in your community. It is a worthy task to continuously seek to live with less stuff, even if it is forced upon you by having a small home!"

To read more about Wendy's and Mikey's adventures, visit their blog at blog.holyscraphotsprings.com, Wendy's website at www.gaiatreehouse.com, and Mikey's website at screwdecaf.cx. Wendy's first book, *The Good Life Lab: Radical Experiments in Living Beyond Money*, was published by Storey Publishing in 2013.

MOBILE HOMES AS TINY HOUSES

The tiny-house movement

Known variously as the "tiny house" or "small house" movement, some families are choosing to buck the trend toward larger and larger homes and are instead opting to live in human-sized dwellings. Even though the houses profiled (averaging about 1,839 square feet) are much larger than the 500-square-foot cutoff the movement currently employs, many believe that the tiny-house movement was initiated by Susan Susanka's 1998 book *The Not So Big House*. Regardless of where the movement began, though, the idea of living in a small house is gaining momentum in homesteading and environmentalist circles and is worth consideration by those interested in voluntary simplicity.

To put the tiny-house movement in perspective, let's look at the changing size of the American home over time. In 1950, the average dwelling clocked in at 983 square feet and sheltered 3.34 people (providing 294 square feet per person). By 2004 the average American's personal space had risen to 914 square feet (a 2,349-square-foot home divided by 2.57 people per household). Those numbers mean that the modern American today has nearly as much space to himself as an entire family did fifty years ago.

These extra-large houses cost us an arm and a leg to build, and many Americans simply assume they have to face thirty years of debt if they want to own their own home. Meanwhile, environmental costs don't stop after the houses are erected (using more than twice the supplies a 1950s home did, of course). In a previous era, owners of large houses closed off portions for the winter, but now most Americans wouldn't dream of having an unheated second story, of moving their workshop to an unfinished barn for summer use, or of keeping their winter clothes in a shed when not in use.

While I find the concept behind the tiny-house movement refreshing, the price tag still gives me sticker shock. One report suggests that the average tiny house costs $20,000 to $50,000 to erect, plus years of labor (since most are owner-built). This book arose out of a wish to suggest a cheaper and more environmentally friendly option for the tiny-house crowd—an old mobile home.

While a trailer can't compete with many tiny houses aesthetically (at least at first), the ecological footprint could be argued to be much lower if you select a mobile home that has already been lived in for forty years and was headed for the dump. Trailers also give budding builders a less daunting project to learn on, provide the flexibility to move your house to a new plot of land, and save a lot of cash in the process. In the end, I believe that if you're aiming for true DIY simplicity, trailersteading is the way to go.

How small is too small?

The term "tiny house" begs the question—how small is too small? I grew up in a 616-square-foot house, which I shared with my parents and two siblings, and I'll admit I felt cramped at times. Meanwhile, a sampling of my blog readers chimed in with their minimum-space requirements, and many of those clocked in right around 150 to 160 square feet per person, which I'll agree is near the dividing line between cramped and manageable. Luckily, most trailers will provide at least this much space as long as your family is no larger than the American norm.

But how do you fit your possessions into such a small domicile if you're used to spreading out across the dozen rooms of a McMansion? While it's easy to advise tiny-house dwellers to "just cut down on the amount of stuff you own," it's actually a bit trickier for an American used to sprawling across a large house to enjoy life in a trailer or tiny house. Here are some tips for making small spaces work for you:

>**Remember economies of scale.** It's easier for two people to live in 300 square feet than for one person to live in 150 square feet because you can double up the bathroom, kitchen, and other communal spaces.

>**Find places to be alone.** I don't think I could have survived in our small house as a teenager if I hadn't enjoyed an outdoor retreat where I spent all of my time between school and supper.

It's good for everyone to have private spaces, even if they're tiny, outdoors, or down at the local coffee shop.

Make every inch count. People who live in small spaces often find ingenious ways to arrange one area so it performs multiple functions. Is your dining table also counter space for meal preparation and a spot for kids to labor over their homework? Does a bathtub in the living room double as a padded bench for company? Can you store seldom-used kitchen appliances on shelves near the ceiling or on hooks attached to the wall? You'll probably need to build many of these double-duty pieces of house-scaping yourself, but that's half the fun.

Take advantage of community buildings. One of our blog readers wrote in to tell me that the trend toward small homes in Japan is mitigated by neighborhood meeting houses, which are used for community gatherings and can also be rented out by individuals. This option is sometimes available in the United States as well; for example, we recently discovered that we have an inexpensive community space nearby where we can put up our guests or host our Thanksgiving dinner. Even though you typically have to pay for these options, the one-time cost is generally cheaper than the ongoing expense of living in a larger home.

Get creative about storage. Many of the things we fill our houses with are just waiting to be used once or twice a year. An unheated, unfinished shed can take a lot of pressure off your inside space—just make sure you don't store anything there that shouldn't be frozen and do keep cloth and food in sealed containers to prevent incursions by mice, ants, and other pests. If you don't have the cash to build a shed and also don't have nosy neighbors, you can follow my mother's lead and store winter clothes in junked cars along your driveway. (Yes, I do come from a long line of permaculture rednecks—reduce, reuse, recycle!)

Sitting under a tin roof during a thunderstorm is one of the simple joys of life.

Enjoy the outdoors. In *The Tiny Book of Tiny Houses*, Lester Walker reports that historically small-house dwellers often moved the toilet, bathing, and kitchen facilities outside. Other parts of the house that can expand into the outdoors include dining and relaxing. We added porches onto our trailer in the summer of 2012, one of which was an 8-foot-by-16-foot roofed space which (including materials and hired labor) cost $950 and was worth every penny. Not only do porches (and gazebos, summer kitchens, etc.) take the pressure off small indoor spaces, they also give you a great opportunity to watch butterflies during lunch and to enjoy the antics of your chickens during dinner. If you need a less permanent space, the big-box stores often sell shade canopies for $100 or less.

Your surroundings make all the difference. If you have the opportunity to buy a homestead, you'll have to make a choice between more land and a larger dwelling. While our trailer would seem excessively cramped if it were located in a trailer park, when surrounded by 58 acres of paradise, it instead feels like a castle. I highly recommend that you do whatever it takes to make your surroundings top-notch so that a tiny house is a place you only want to retreat to during cold winter nights and drizzly days.

These tips aside, it's worth looking at a tiny house as an asset rather than as an inconvenience—many people move to small spaces precisely because the reduced quarters require inhabitants to simplify their lives. "Divesting as much of our rarely-used space and getting into a right-sized space was one of our top motivations when we moved out of our house and into our trailer," wrote one of my RV-dwelling friends. Take his advice and don't be afraid of a small space—the economic, environmental, and psychological rewards are more than worth it.

Living large in a small space

Maggie Turner puts her furniture on wheels to make each piece do double duty in a small space.

"One thing I find makes living in small spaces easier to deal with is to put casters on most of the furniture, making it simple to move around to suit the occasion. For example, the computer work station gets moved nearer the masonry heater in the winter, because it is much colder by the exterior walls and windows. In the warmer weather, it gets moved near the windows to enjoy the view while working. The computer is also the entertainment center, and it can be moved for viewing from wherever we are sitting.

"Another thing we find is that, when people visit, there is not enough seating since we only have seating for two. Folding camping chairs have come to the rescue. When people drop by we bring out the folding chairs and the little living room has instant seating for guests." —Maggie Turner

"My husband and I lived for 12 years in an 800-square-foot house—it was very cozy and I loved it. It was great for keeping down buying because there was no space to put new things. The rule was if a new book came in, an old book had to leave. We had potlucks in the summer when we could sit everyone on the porch. We also had a barn for storing tools, bikes, building supplies, etc., so that helped. We moved two years ago next door to a bigger house, not because of the size but because of the great southern exposure (and greenhouse). I miss the coziness of our small house."
—Katherine

"The secret to living in a small house is not to clutter it up, in my opinion. Look for clever solutions to store stuff without having it all over the place. For example, a thin plate of plywood fixed parallel to the wall with a hinge is invisible when closed, yet has room to hang a lot of tools on the inside."
—Roland Smith

Realities of life in a tiny house

While the previous sections probably made many large-house dwellers dream of the joys of tiny-house living, I don't want readers to come away with a purely rose-tinted view of trailer life. So I'll share a bit of the flip side of the coin—small-space realities that might not be quite your style.

Wall space is functional rather than aesthetic in a tiny house.

There are no public spaces in your house. Those of you who live in large houses probably don't pay much attention to the way your residence has public spaces where you don't mind inviting strangers in, as well as private spaces like your bedroom. Tiny houses double up functions, which tends to make all spaces feel private (at least to a shy introvert). Solution: Build a nice porch and only invite people over in the summer. Silver lining: Small spaces feel cozy during the 99 percent of the time that you spend at home with only your family around.

Only one person can move around in a room at a time. Small spaces mean that you need to find a spot to settle into once you're inside, then stay there. Solution: I have no clue how families with rowdy kids handle this, but for Mark and me, it generally means treating the trailer like a time-share—when I'm cooking, he stays out of the kitchen, and vice versa when the dishes are being done. Silver lining: You can imagine how accidentally impinging on your spouse's personal space inevitably adds to marital harmony.

Walls are not for art. Chances are, you'll need every speck of wall space for some combination of windows, shelves, and hanging things. Solution: Maybe the art should go in the outhouse? Silver lining: It's much easier to keep your life relatively simple if you look at all of your accumulated possessions every day.

Your smoke detector will go off at least once a week. Even the best smoke detectors are designed for larger residences, so chances are good you'll set off false alarms quite frequently. Deglazing a greasy pan for easier cleanup inevitably sets off our smoke detector, as does roasting vegetables under the broiler. Solution: Learn the right doors and windows to open when broiling to prevent the klaxon and move your smoke detector as far as possible from the kitchen. Silver lining: You don't need to worry about your smoke detector running out of batteries without you noticing.

Did you notice how each unfortunate reality came with a silver lining? That's one of the joys of trailersteading—a few unconventional techniques are all it takes to make tiny-house dwelling fun!

Case study: A retro trailer

Miles enjoys the simplicity of his 1955 Spartan Imperial Mansion.

Photo credit: Miles Flansburg

When asked how he feels about his trailer, Miles Flansburg said, "We love it!" He and his family live near Denver in a modern American home, but they bought a 1955 Spartan Imperial Mansion to place on their land in Wyoming, which Miles gets to visit for a week per month. He found the 8-by-42-foot trailer for $5,500, spent another $1,000 fixing it up, and now has a free place to stay during his time off.

Trailer parks are a good place to find old trailers at a low price.

"I was looking for a quick, cheap, easy shelter and I found this trailer on Craigslist," Miles explained. "My wife agreed to it. The kids really do not care. It allowed us to have a nice little shelter on our land. We would still be camping in a tent if not for the trailer. And in this area, bears and lions are a concern."

Smaller trailers are much easier to transport to a new home.

When asked about the advantages of trailer life, Miles focused on the basics—a quick, cheap living space that's easy to clean. He also mentioned that having such a small home tempts you to spend more time outside, turning your life into "a big camping trip," with the trailer simply being a place to eat and sleep.

Photo credit: Miles Flansburg

Small kitchens are one disadvantage that can be remedied with careful renovation.

Miles had a long history of living in mobile homes, so he knew what to expect. As a child, his family sometimes lived in rental trailers and Miles said, "I did feel a little less worthy about myself. The 'American Dream' is a powerful force. But I do not remember anyone else making me feel bad."

Photo credit: Miles Flansburg

A trailer allowed Miles to spend more time on his land with little fuss.

As an adult, he and his family have used trailers as transition housing during moves. "We would rent a trailer and then take our time finding the right home to live in. We would pack up everything but the basics and put that in storage. It seemed like a much simpler life, but we are all so used to bigger homes that it is a big change from one to another. I personally would not mind living more simply, but my family is used to having more room. After living in large homes, it is hard to get used to the smaller space. You really have to economize your stuff."

Photo credit: Miles Flansburg

Trailers tempt their inhabitants to spend more time enjoying the outdoors.

Although Miles tends to call his trailer a "cottage" or "camper," he hasn't found much stigma attached to the lifestyle. "The old Spartans are actually pretty retro and romantic," he said, then went on to mention the online community of people who collect, restore, and live in Spartan trailers (autos.groups.yahoo.com/group/Spartantrailercoaches/). Internet friendships have definitely made Miles's adventure much easier and more fun.

DISADVANTAGES OF TRAILER HOMESTEADING

Why we don't all live in trailers

I love my trailer—sometimes I feel like nicknaming the structure Independence because of all the life choices that our living space has simplified. However, when I put the question out to my blog readers asking them to comment on why they wouldn't want to live in a trailer, many valid points came streaming back to me. The quotes in the following sections come from those homesteaders or homesteaders-to-be, plus my mother (Adrianne), father (Errol), and mother-in-law (Rose Nell).

Luckily, most of the negative points of trailer life can be worked around with careful renovations or can be re-envisioned in a positive light. Later chapters give tips on rehabbing trailers, but I also include some pointers in the sections that follow for taking lemons and making lemonade.

Fire

> Sara: I notice a lot of people are worried about safety, and that's one of my biggest concerns, too. I don't know a lot about design differences in trailers, but my dad has worked in construction for over 30 years and was impressed with our 1998 model that is made out of a pretty standard wall construction—wooden studs with fiberglass insulation and fire-resistant sheetrock on the inside. There's a lot of plywood, but I don't think our place is too much more flammable than the typical stick-frame house. The fact that it is off the ground would probably feed a lot more oxygen into a fire, though.

> Errol: When you mentioned getting a trailer to live in, my first concern was for the many trailer-fire deaths in the area. Trailers are built using extremely inflammable substances and people have less than three minutes to get out if there is a fully involved fire. Because older trailers are built with two-inch walls, they are expensive to heat using their original electric furnaces. So many folks install

wood or coal stoves, often in the cheapest way, leading to a high death rate from fires. So I urged you to not do this.

Michelle: I remember learning in fire-safety courses that from the point of ignition to there being nothing left but the steel frame underneath is three minutes when a trailer burns.

The most-feared aspect of living in a mobile home is fire. Although the three-minutes-to-complete-destruction figure bandied about doesn't seem to have a basis in the literature, mobile home fires are more likely to result in mortality than fires in a more traditional house. The 1979 US government document *Mobile Home Fire Studies: Summary and Recommendations* reported that although "the incidence rate was approximately the same, the injury and life hazard and the extent of property damage per incident were three to five times greater [for mobile homes] than for conventional residences." In other words, you're no more likely to have a fire in your mobile home, but the average mobile-home fire is more costly to possessions and life than is the average house fire.

Before I delve into the problems associated with mobile homes and fire (and how you can prevent your trailer from burning down), it's worth backing up and understanding house fires in general. In most cases, residential fires are localized and small—perhaps a pan of hot grease goes up in flames, you throw baking soda on the fire, and the problem is resolved. The danger is that a small fire can spread to nearby objects and to the structure of the house itself, a phase known as flashover, at which point heat and gases can cause death if you don't exit quickly.

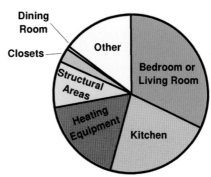

Cigarette smoking igniting bedding or sofas was the leading cause of mobile-home fires in the 1979 study, with range-related kitchen fires following close behind.

Assuming you don't smoke, most fires start in the kitchen. In mobile homes, these range fires reach the flashover stage quickly since there is usually a flammable cabinet directly above the stove. I think this is where the three-minute figure comes from since the report cited above concludes: "Without a metal range hood, sustained burning of the Class C cabinet underside occurred within three minutes after ignition in the majority of tests with a cooking oil fire."

Luckily, there are some pretty simple steps that mobile-home dwellers can take to ensure that a fire on the stove doesn't burn their trailer down. The study mentioned above recommends adding a range hood located at least two feet above the stove top and extending at least five inches forward past the edge of the cabinet, with a quarter inch or thicker piece of flame-resistant material sandwiched between the underside of the cabinet and the range hood. Cabinets within eighteen inches horizontal distance of the stove top should also have a flame-resistant bottom added, and the same material can be used to fireproof the wall behind the stove. Alternatively, you can go a step further and coat these surfaces with stainless steel sheets, backed with nonflammable insulation, an option that is not only fireproof but is also easy to clean. These measures will give you more time to put out a fire in the ignition stage, which can protect your possessions and life.

Another problem with mobile homes is the particleboard interior walls, which tend to be quite flammable. If you can afford it, this is another good place to start your renovations, replacing the current siding with a material in the NFPA or IBC class A, which will have a flame spread index (FSI) below 25. Options include gypsum wallboard, gypsum sheeting (a.k.a. drywall), fiber-cement board, inorganic-reinforced-cement board, or fire-retardant-treated plywood (although the last may cause some outgassing). With a 4-foot-by-8-foot sheet of drywall currently costing $10, replacing the walls and ceiling in a medium-sized mobile home won't break the bank (although it might break your back).

Of course, all of the traditional fire-safety tips also apply. Install smoke detectors and change their batteries regularly, keep the appropriate type of fire extinguishers near the stove and know how to use them, and have a fire-escape plan that everyone in the family knows and understands. Never leave stoves, candles, or other potential fire hazards unattended, and keep heaters a safe distance away from flammable objects. With those fire-prevention measures in place, along with retrofits to the most problematic features of mobile homes, you should be as safe—or safer—than someone living in a traditional house who never checks the batteries in their smoke detector.

Chemical offgassing

Michelle: The main reason I won't live in one now, though, is the chemical offgassing. Trailers have a distinct smell. I know that as they age it supposedly gets better, but the trailer my parents bought in 1984 STILL has the same smell as the day we brought it home. It may be milder, but it's still there. There is a high incidence of cancer on both sides of my family, and I do everything I know how to take care of my body and prevent that dreadful disease.

Another common fear associated with mobile homes is that chemicals offgassed by the construction materials will make you sick. This is a very valid concern for new trailers, but the older trailers you'll find free or cheap have already lost most or all of the harmful chemicals.

For example, particleboard emits formaldehyde, which has a half-life of around six years (shorter in hot, damp areas and longer in cold, dry areas). Those of you who remember your high-school chemistry will recall that a half-life simply refers to the length of time required for half of the chemicals to dissipate or break down. So, after a trailer is six years old, half of the formaldehyde is gone; at twelve years old, three quarters (half plus half of a half) is gone; at eighteen years old, 87.5 percent is gone; and at twenty-four years old, 93.75 percent is gone. Free trailers are often thirty or forty years old, at which point levels of hazardous chemicals will be extremely low.

If you stumble across a newer mobile home at a low price, some experts suggest that you might be able to bake out the harmful chemicals. Find somewhere else to live for a couple of days while you turn on the heat to raise the interior trailer temperature to 90 degrees Fahrenheit. Then open all the windows and use fans to push air out. The technique is somewhat controversial, but it shouldn't hurt (although it might melt your candles and will definitely raise your heating bill).

While you're at it, you should be very careful of new materials you put back into any living space. The new-paint smell is a sign of outgassing and you'll also be introducing chemicals to your home on particleboard, wood stains, carpets, synthetic fibers, and foams. As with the formaldehyde issue, older is safer, so reclaimed wood from a deconstruction zone and old furniture from the thrift store is not only cheaper, it's also better for your health.

Lack of insulation

> *Rebecca: My main complaint with our early 1980s mobile home is keeping it comfortable in extreme weather. We (not so affectionately) call it our "tin can." The metal siding acts as a miserable heat conductor . . . cooking us in the summer sun and then whisking away the warmth in the winter.*

If you unscrew the siding on most mobile homes, you'll see that the walls are built with two-by-twos instead of two-by-four studs and the ceiling is probably framed with two-by-fours instead of with deeper lumber. These smaller-than-usual cavities keep the weight of the trailer at a minimum so you can transport it to its new home, but they also prevent the inclusion of much insulation. This isn't one of those lemonade issues—a later chapter will suggest several methods you can use to insulate a mobile home so it no longer has the tin-can effect. And if you're in a hurry, check out the case study "Building a house for your trailer."

Case study: Building a house for your trailer

Will's travel trailer outlived his marriage and first farm. He and his trailer are pictured here in their new location.

Will spent nearly three years in his 32-foot Fire Ball trailer. "[My wife and I] were living in a condo at Shilshole Bay in Seattle when the nesting urge overcame us and we decided to have a house built out on a 6.5-acre piece of property we owned overlooking the Snoqualmie River Valley near Carnation," Will began. "As the house design became grander and the engineering requirements from the county more onerous, we realized that we would have to begin an austerity program during the build. With our backgrounds well steeped in outdoor living and roughing it in general, we soon came to agreement that to park a travel trailer on the property would be perfect in all respects. We would save money on housing, we would be near to the construction site, and we would be living out in the forest. Perfect!"

Will's favorite aspects of living in his travel trailer included the low cost and the foresty feeling of residing in the woods.

Will and his wife enjoyed many facets of the trailer life, but the move was a shock in other ways. The biggest problem was keeping the uninsulated space warm with only propane, since their farm was off-grid. Will had a solution, though: "Having read a lot about passive-solar home design over the years, we decided to build an envelope around the trailer based on an easily erectable metal carport. That winter we lived with only the roof of the carport protecting us and dressed warmly while at home."

To keep the trailer warm, Will erected a passive-solar shell around it.

Photo credit: Will

"But in our second summer, disaster struck when my wife was diagnosed with cancer," Will continued. "The house was lagging way behind schedule, winter loomed, and trips to the hospital became a way of life as she underwent chemo, then radiation. She took a leave from her job and I struggled to keep her warm up there all alone during the days while I worked."

A wood stove in the carport and a propane sailboat heater in the trailer made life more comfortable.

Photo credit: Will

"First of all, I built walls into the 16-by-40-foot carport with glass windows along the south side and insulation on the north. Then I installed a small propane sailboat fireplace heater vented through the trailer and carport roofs, and also fashioned a vent for the trailer's forced air and water heaters. This created a still-air envelope around the trailer and helped significantly to keep things warm inside . . . but not warm enough. So I got an older wood stove and installed it in one corner of the enclosed carport. This really helped and often I could fire up the wood stove and turn off all the trailer heaters during the night."

Unfortunately, his wife's worsening condition eventually forced the pair to sell their newly constructed house (which they had never had the opportunity to live in), but Will was able to pull his trailer back to town as a consolation prize. By 2012, his wife was doing well, but the pair had split up and Will had found another farm. He lived in his Fire Ball while cleaning up the current farmhouse and still keeps the trailer around for guests.

All told, the heating improvements in the Fire Ball's original location cost $2,700, which included $1,200 for the carport, $500 for lumber, insulation, and glass to enclose it, $800 for the sailboat heater, and $200 for the wood stove. While Will's choice might not have been the cheapest option, it was a quick-and-dirty solution during a crisis situation, and the carport could have become a shop or extra living space had everything gone as planned with their original house build.

No basement

Deb: The one reason I would not want to live in a trailer is that it doesn't have a basement. Growing up in Texas where tornadoes are a regular fact of life and basements can save lives, and then moving to New England where every house had a basement which, depending on the home, could be used for cool storage of food, or act as a cooler sleeping area in the hot, humid summer (few in New England have air conditioning), I would be at a loss without that very important part of the house. Ok, that was a really long sentence, but basements seem to somehow connect the house as part of the land, and I would feel too "temporary" in a mobile home.

Lack of a basement is a definite disadvantage of the mobile home. Of course, many traditional homes lack basements too, and a stand-alone root cellar actually preserves food better than a basement connected to a house. But those who wish for a basement can go the extra step to build one under their trailer—see the case study "An incognito trailer" for more information.

Long-term cost

Errol: Over a period of years, I've observed people add onto their trailers with new roofs, new rooms, etc., until a stick-built house surrounds the original trailer. This is done as the trailer seems less adequate for its occupants. For both cost and quality reasons, it makes more sense to design a house for the long haul, one that can be built by modules as need requires and money allows. Designing with your needs, heating efficiency, and landscape in mind will end up with a much better fit than retrofitting around an in-adequately-designed trailer.

Another important issue with trailers is their economic consequences. A local economy benefits when a local product is taken as close to a finished product as possible. Compared to local stick building, which employs relatively skilled workers in the community at a decent wage, trailers drain local money out of the community to a centralized location where more money goes to corporate profits. So trailers are, initially, a drain on the local economy. The drain isn't just the lack of labor income. It includes a loss to local building suppliers, and all the support industry surrounding home construction. Secondhand trailers, of course, are a different matter.

Although my father's figures sound realistic on the surface, I think that most people who compare building a new home to renovating an existing space don't include all of the embedded costs into the former endeavor. Let's say you're going to build a small straw-bale home for your family, planning to take the year off and use your own elbow-grease to keep the cost down to include only the $50,000 worth of supplies. You sign a 30-year mortgage to make that happen (meaning you'll add an extra $30,000 to the cost in interest payments), you take a year off work (perhaps a $40,000 loss depending on your salary), and you have to continue to rent for a year ($16,000) while making your dream a reality. The total price tag of that home comes to $136,000.

On the other hand, the trailersteaders interviewed in this book have proven that you can move into a very nice trailer nearly immediately for $22,000 or less. David and Mary's incognito trailer (profiled later), with a full basement, roof, extensive insulation, and general impression of being a modern stick-built home, cost about $40,000 (in today's dollars) to buy, install, and renovate, giving the couple extra cash to spend on solar panels and a windmill.

These figures mean you'd be saving 84 percent by moving into a nice trailer now, and perhaps 71 percent over your lifetime if you continue to improve your trailer into a top-notch home. Even if you compare these trailer costs to a tiny-house builder who paid for everything up front and did the construction on weekends, so he only spent $50,000 on his house, the renovated trailer comes out ahead.

As a final note in favor of a trailer, there's no danger of losing it all when times get tough if you pay as you go. Don't trailers look like a better investment now?

Depreciation and impermanence

Heather W: I would certainly live in [a mobile home], but, given options, I would not choose one as my permanent residence because of their "throw-away" nature. What I mean by this is that where I live (Canada), they are not a good investment at all and are looked upon as temporary. You cannot easily get financing for them and often, they have to be replaced . . . Their value does not appreciate. A well-built home can withstand the test of time, over hundreds of years.

Adrianne: I have changed in how I relate to your living in a trailer. At first, I looked on it as temporary, and thought you might want to start building your own "permanent" house. Now, I realize that lots of places people live in are temporary, even if they own them. For people's lives do change.

Photo credit: Rose Nell Hamilton and Jayne Wead

Rose Nell's three rental trailers.

For another perspective, I dropped an email to my mother-in-law, Rose Nell, who owns three trailers in southeastern Kentucky. She lived in one of the mobile homes for several years, now rents out all three, and is looking to sell them. Rose Nell wrote to me about the disadvantages of trailers that aren't your primary residence:

> *In hindsight, a trailer depreciates with every passing year. It makes it hard to get proper insurance to cover all expenses if something bad happens.*
>
> *With a stick house, everything one does to improve the house makes it increase in value, and even if you do nothing to improve, it appreciates.*
>
> *If I had all the money that I have invested into these trailers at the beginning, I would not have rehabbed, but rather invested in something that would appreciate in value. But we are back at the beginning again. No money, looking for my space. Trailers big or small can be the answer.*

This is a fascinating issue, and one where I feel the average homesteader has a long way to go in breaking free of the mainstream American conception of the home as an appreciable asset. We are indoctrinated to believe that we need to build up our credit so we can "buy" a house (mortgaged, of course), which is likely to become our single biggest asset. We spend our lives improving the worth of that structure, hoping that we'll be able to sell it for more than we put into it when we need cash at a later date, and we pay insurance companies 0.35 percent of the house's value each year to protect that investment.

The lifestyle I advocate requires an abrupt about-face from that traditional point of view. Rather than wishing that your home appreciated, I advocate choosing a spot and sinking down roots so you never want to sell. Put money in the bank for those worst-case-scenario periods (or buy land or gold if you're worried about our banking system), then start your housing with something you can afford—a free or very cheap trailer. Pay as you go with improvements, learning building skills in the process and making your home as livable as possible without pouring too much of your blood, sweat, and tears into the process. Be happy when your home depreciates because that means your property taxes are lower and you are that much more independent of the mainstream economy. Consider following the lead of the Mayans and intentionally under-building, then replace your living area every fifty-two years (or at whatever interval appeals to you).

For those who aren't quite as radical as I am, you can head back for some more expert advice from my mother-in-law:

> Now if a person, such as me, really wanted to improve on the saleability of my lot with three trailers to make it more easily financed and insurable (meaning the buyer could get financing), I could surrender the certificate of title. There is a process that is backed by Fannie Mae and handled through the states wherein if the manufactured home is attested to be permanently affixed to the land, the trailer can be considered a conversion of the home as an improvement to the real estate upon which it is located.

The certificate of title to the manufactured home must be sur-rendered at the time when the affidavit is filed. The county clerk must not accept the surrender of a certificate of title that shows an unreleased lien unless it is accompanied by a release of such lien. When the county clerk files the affida-vit, he or she must provide a copy to the property valuation administrator for inclusion in the county real-property tax rolls. Hence, one's property taxes will increase with that inclusion!

The choice is yours—turn your trailer into a home and let it appre-ciate, or take advantage of the low property taxes of a depreciating dwelling. Either way, trailers have the flexibility to suit your lifestyle.

Aesthetics

Faith: We've considered a trailer for our future homestead. Here is why we decided against it (for now): My husband is a carpenter who has been building/remodeling his own homes since he was in his twenties. He's very artistic and prefers buildings that are inspiring. And he works for food and beer. If I wasn't married to a fantastic (and visionary) carpenter, I would probably opt for the trailer. But if we can have a larger space for only a little more money, why not go for it?

Heather W: I like a good design, pleasing to the eye, and trailers are usually just a long rectangle, rather banal.

Adrianne: About aesthetics: I was sort of put off by so much non-wood, also by seemingly a very little bedroom for you. This year, with your porches and the barn fixed, your whole potential has changed.

My husband and I take a lot of photos and share them with readers on our blog, and I'll admit that I often frame my shots so that our trailer is out of sight. On the other hand, some trailer-dwellers have gone to extremes to make their trailer look just as beautiful on the outside as the average house, and simply adding a couple of porches to our trailer has definitely changed the aesthetic of our domicile dramatically.

Later chapters will provide in-depth tips for remodeling a trailer, and it wouldn't hurt to follow Rebecca's lead (profiled in the case study below) to integrate your mobile home into the landscape. But there's also something to be said for learning to enjoy what you have. As Michelle explains below, there's a lot to love about a trailer:

> *I grew up in house trailers. I actually love them on an emotional level. They feel more homey to me. I also love that they are designed so smartly! Every single inch of space is utilized in the trailers I've been around. I love that. It seems that stick-built homes often are built with lots of wasted space. My ideal would be to have a stick-built home made from the designs of a house trailer.*

Case study: Hiding in the vegetation

Rebecca added a trellis to one side of her trailer to "distract and create a focal point."

Photo credit: Rebecca

If you don't have a lot of cash to throw at a remodeling project, plants can make a huge difference in the exterior appearance of a trailer. Rebecca had three goals in her landscaping endeavors—to shade the mobile home during the summer, to screen the blocky shape of the structure, and to provide useful food.

"I let the bamboo on the other side of our house escape the nursery pots they came in, so now we have a thicket going, which I will eventually thin," wrote Rebecca.

She started by placing fast-growing trees around the perimeter of the house. "I am really glad I chose a horse chestnut tree, as it has grown very quickly and should be great for shade," Rebecca noted. Since she and her husband added a foundation to their trailer, they were also careful to keep the trees "a reasonable distance away, because tree roots will eventually crack the foundation if planted too close. And also because whenever you work on the outside, you want some wiggle room."

The bamboo and trellis pictured above did a great job breaking up the rectangular shape of the trailer. "I've also let stinging nettle grow in there (it volunteered), which is a great food source in spring. The back of our house faces west and that is where we need the most shade, but we have only just decided to build a system of trellises and grow probably 5 or 6 grape vines. I have to be a little more careful landscaping that area because the septic is behind the house on one side and also some of my vegetable garden, which I don't want to shade too much."

Rebecca's experience inspired me so much that I began to follow her lead. Skip ahead to the section "Shade trellis to cool your home with plants" to see our own experiments with using vines to block the summer sun.

Zoning

Sara: I live in a pretty rural area and lots of people here live in trailers. Some people (families, small ethnic enclaves, other low-income communities) squeeze trailers on one spot of land like a game of Tetris. With that, there's the valid issue of safety, but there's also so much prejudice and it has definitely seeped into our local planning and zoning discussions.

I attended one local planning meeting where I was just appalled at the blatant discrimination against people in trailers. The firm hired to help put the plan together actually pointed out that the punishments that were being proposed were discriminatory. A few examples: trailer communities have to be screened from public view by vegetation or privacy fences and all trailers must have skirting even when they can't be seen from the road, in order to complete all the permitting processes. At one point the planner rolled her eyes about complaints and said "Oh come on, this isn't going to break anyone's wallet. A piece of lattice is $20. They can just buy it and slap it on. No one is going to suffer." Ha-ha! As if one piece of lattice would do the job of skirting an entire trailer.

Now that's better than those communities where trailers aren't even allowed—but these are becoming increasingly

*common too. A tiny little city just north of me has already
outlawed trailers within the city limits, including very nice,
modern double-wides. That's ridiculous.*

*Ultimately, mobile-home manufacturers and other pro-
ponents of manufactured housing have been strong
advocates against housing discrimination. In the example
above, the LA firm's representative pointed out that any
ordinances that specifically target people living in trailers
and not people in houses is unlawful. Skirting, for example, would have to apply to stick-built homes as well. That
means all of those people who like the southern look of
houses on piers would have to conceal their open under-
parts, too. Still, local governments can often find some
ways around federal housing laws, and it's probably going
to be more and more challenging to find a place where you
can move your trailer, even if you own the land.*

Unfortunately, there's not much to say about the zoning issue, which
is related to the stigma problem outlined in a later section. On the other
hand, you might want to think twice about moving to an area that
has zoning restrictions outlawing mobile homes. These same upscale
communities are likely to have neighborhood covenants requiring you
to dry your clothes inside rather than hanging them on a line and
are unlikely to be thrilled if you bring home a milk goat. In contrast,
poverty-stricken regions allow you the freedom to choose your own
homesteading adventure, and even if your politics don't line up with
those of your neighbors, you can probably learn to get along. Check out
the section on choosing an ugly-duckling property for more information.

Trailer parks

*Rose Nell: Living in a trailer park, even if you own your
trailer you are living in, you have to pay to lease the land,
pay utilities, and in some cases park permits and fees.*

Not only do expenses add up when living in a trailer park, most independent-minded folks just don't enjoy the experience of living cheek-to-jowl with so many neighbors. In a pinch, you can build community wherever you're at, but all of the trailersteaders I've interviewed hauled their trailers out of the park ASAP and I recommend you do the same.

Just think, if your house is essentially free, you might be able to afford quite a bit of land, especially if you choose an ugly-duckling property. I can attest to the fact that trailer-hauling companies can pull a trailer up a steep mountainside, across a creek, through miles of mud, and into just about any location imaginable.

Social stigma

> *Adrianne: I think it is true, at least from what I've read of people who live in trailers in Maine (and probably in New Hampshire), that the school-age kids from trailers are more looked down on. The term "double-wide" is pejorative, in some people's mouths: people make fun of them for boasting that they live in a double-wide.*

> *Rose Nell: The stigma we hear of is "trailer trash," which stems from ignorance of those who do not respect other people in any facet of life that one does not agree. I have always heard of row houses (older duplexes found in the low-rent districts of different cities), being said in a negative manner as well.*

Are you trailer trash if you live in a trailer? Perusing the words of the many trailer-dwellers I interviewed, I began to realize that there are a couple of facets of trailer-life that may cause your community to look down upon you. Counterintuitively, mobile homes have more stigma among the lower-middle class and the upper-lower class than among people who come from more money. I suspect this is related to the way I enjoyed running around barefoot as a child but my husband's aunt was always careful to don shoes—she didn't want anyone to think she couldn't afford appropriate footwear, while my mother (raised in the middle class) wasn't afraid of the stigma.

Voluntary simplicity in general is better received among the upper classes, who want to return to a simpler lifestyle, than by people struggling to ensure that their children enjoy easier lives than they had. For example, Deb, the mother of Mikey (profiled in the "Cheap and green" section), was firm in her avoidance of the trailer stigma:

> In short, "NO," I never felt that they were "moving down" to trailer living. My husband David and I were very excited that they were taking this opportunity to follow their dream. If anything, I envy their lifestyle and sometimes wish I could start again and live like them.

As an adult, you can generally choose to socialize with people who respect your efforts toward simple living, but children are more likely to bear the brunt of class-based discrimination. Any form of simple living, from trailersteading to growing your own vegetables, will have a similar effect. For example, as a teenager, I was leery of bringing friends to our home, which was a traditional, cinder-block house, but which was much smaller and less expensively furnished than the homes of other students in my classes. On the other hand, despite some teen angst at being forced to live within my parents' ethics, I'm now very grateful that I was raised simply since the experience made me less fearful of tightening my belt on my own path to homestead independence.

On the other hand, if you're not willing to thumb your nose at the world, there's another alternative—blend in. A trailer can be renovated to look just like a stick-built home, and even without fancy additions, a well-manicured lawn and flowerbeds can appeal to the neighbors if you want to go that route. Keep reading for tips on turning your trailer into a beautiful domicile in later chapters.

FINDING AND MOVING TO THE LAND

Case study: Trailer park to woodland paradise
Stepping-stone trailer

Jonathan and Andrea bought a mobile home in a trailer park, where they lived for two years while searching for the perfect tract of land.

Jonathan and Andrea Combs are thirty-somethings who used a trailer as a stepping stone on their journey out of the city. "We spent the first ten years of our married life living in various rented apartments, a townhouse, and even one 'real' house," Andrea explained. "We had decided that the city we were living in was getting too big and, to live a more sustainable life, and for our sanity, we needed to get out into the 'country.' We soon realized that finding both a house and a piece of land that we liked together was going to be impossible. So we decided to focus on the land and build a house."

Jonathan chimed in: "Andrea had previously indicated that she was not interested in living in a trailer, but when we decided to move to the country, it seemed like a good option and she agreed."

"Building a house was going to take time, and even longer if we were not living on site," continued Andrea. "We looked into small pre-built sheds, yurts, small cabins, etc. But none seemed right for our lifestyle and environment. So we decided to buy a trailer, live in it till we found land and had the trailer paid off, then move it to the land."

Jonathan and Andrea tore out the carpeting . . .

. . . and added laminate flooring and a paint job to improve the interior space.

The duo found the perfect trailer for $8,000 in a trailer park with a lot fee of $215 per month. The 1982 model was old but in good condition, with 924 square feet of interior space broken up into two bedrooms, two baths, a kitchen, and a sunken living room.

Rather than beginning construction on a house as soon as they purchased their new property, the couple was able to transfer their trailer to its new location and move right in.

Jonathan and Andrea appreciated the ability to move out of their apartment and into the trailer immediately. Two years later, the perfect 32-acre property came along and they spent an additional $12,000 having a spot graded for the trailer on their new land, installing a septic tank, and having the trailer delivered and set up. "[The trailer] allowed us to save money on housing while we searched for the property," Jonathan said, "and now allows us to take our time with choosing the spot on our property for building the type of home we wish to construct, while also allowing us to build at our own pace."

Energy efficiency

"I feel it is better to be reusing a home than to build a traditional house," Andrea said. "We still hope to build a natural home someday. But even then we will use the trailer as a guest house or a house for my in-laws."

"The primary reason for wanting to build a house is the increased efficiency, especially of a house designed with passive-solar principles," Jonathan added. "If comparing homes of equal size, I would say a trailer is probably worse for the environment, as a traditional house should provide increased energy efficiency and should last longer. However, trailers do have several environmental advantages, in my opinion.

"First is that most are smaller than the average house. Second is that a trailer can be moved to a new location if desired rather than torn down and replaced if the owners of the land want something different. Lastly, due to the shape and layout of a single-wide trailer, it is easier to use natural lighting throughout the house, and to get some added heat from southern windows. This isn't as easy with wider houses, or houses with rooms separated from southern windows by a wall."

Changing the orientation of the trailer and adding a porch to shade the largest window in the summer increased the thermal efficiency of Jonathan and Andrea's trailer.

While waiting for a more traditional house to materialize in their minds (and wallets), Jonathan and Andrea are still finding ways to make their trailer more energy efficient. When they moved their home out of the trailer park, they reoriented the structure so that the long side with the largest windows faced south for passive-solar heating in the winter. A porch roof on that side prevents summer sun from baking the trailer.

The new orientation also corrected a problem that the pair noticed while living in the trailer park—the south-facing bedroom "would get incredibly hot during the daytime." That bedroom now points east, so they enjoy morning sun without the space heating up unduly during the day.

Andrea, who is "an avid crafter and upcycler," made insulated coverings for many of the windows, which she reports really help with heating and cooling. "We replaced the appliances with energy-star-rated ones," she adds, rounding out their low cost, but effective, energy improvements.

Would you take a dream home?

An artistic paint job spices up the master bedroom.

I asked each of the interviewed trailer-dwellers the same question: "If you were offered a 'dream home,' at least the American average of 2,700 square feet, brand new, for free (but you would be responsible for taxes, upkeep, etc., and couldn't just sell it and live on the proceeds), would you take it?" Unsurprisingly, many would have leapt at the hypothetical offer, but Andrea and Jonathan were more hesitant.

"For me that would all come down to the location," Andrea responded. "If it were in a subdivision in a city, no way. If it were to be installed on my lot, I might."

Jonathan was even more leery. "If it were a standard house, then no, I would not take it. Especially if it were located in a subdivision. Even if the house would be built on my own property, I would not take it, as part of the reason for choosing to live in a trailer was to give us the flexibility to build our own dream house. If the dream home could be built to my specifications, and could be significantly smaller than the 2,700 square feet, I would take it, but otherwise I prefer living in the trailer until we can build what we want."

Social consequences and advice for others

The stepping-stone trailer is a pleasant home for now.

Although Andrea and Jonathan are aware of the stigma attached to trailer dwelling, neither felt that their housing choice impacted their life in any way. "I gave up worrying about what my family thought of me when I quit a good job to stay at home," Andrea said. "This is just another in the long list of reasons they think I am odd." In fact, she enjoyed the way the trailer "forces us to live simply, deliberately, thinking about what we have, what we need."

"If living in a trailer is a stepping stone to living your dream life, do not let the perception of others keep you from achieving that dream," Jonathan admonished. Those of us interested in living a more deliberate life would do well to follow his lead.

To read more about Jonathan's and Andrea's adventures, visit Jonathan's blog at www.simplelivingcomplexworld.blogspot.com.

The ugly-duckling property

Jonathan and Andrea's story suggests another reason for a potential homesteader to choose the trailer life—flexibility. Although urban homesteading has its own appeal, many wannabe farmers dream of finding a rural acreage where they can spread out, plant trees, graze sheep, and do as they wish. If you don't already live in the region where you want to settle, though, the hunt for land can be expensive and time-consuming. Why not buy a cheap trailer nearby to expedite your land search, then move your house onto your new farm as a starter dwelling, or as your permanent accommodation?

Although the hunt for property is really beyond the scope of this book, I can't resist making a few suggestions you aren't likely to hear anywhere else. In this case, my advice can be boiled down to the following—choose an ugly-duckling property. You will probably have a very specific vision by the time you reach the land-hunting stage, and for many of us that vision includes a well-insulated but quirky house, extensive pastures, a mature orchard, prime garden soil, a pastoral view, and so forth. However, most new homesteaders aren't actually ready to dive into a fully-formed farm and will instead discover that their beautiful property turns into an exhausting place to spend all weekend mowing, interspersed with long hours spent working in town to pay down the mortgage.

On the other hand, if you apply the same simple-living philosophy to your land search as you did to your housing search, you may be able to purchase a less-than-perfect property outright, quit your job, and devote your time to building your homesteading paradise. As the ugly-duckling property fledges into a beautiful swan, you'll have the added bonus of knowing that it follows your own template at your own pace, rather than someone else's. Plus, it's immensely satisfying to take a waterlogged marsh or rundown hillside and turn that land into a green, vibrant garden or pasture, knowing that every fruit that comes off your grapevines is due to the labor of your own two hands.

Of course, not every ugly-duckling property is worth even a low price tag. The trick to selecting an ugly-duckling property that doesn't stay ugly forever is figuring out which major inconveniences you can live with and even enjoy, and which ones are real deal breakers. Each imperfection you accept will not only mean a lower asking price, but will almost certainly equate to lower property taxes later. Here are some ideas to get you started on your hunt:

Although we usually opt to stay home when the floodwaters rise, sometimes we're forced to gear up or strip down to get across.

Problematic access. To reach our farm, we have to walk through a third of a mile of floodplain, which includes a creek crossing that floods over my head a few times a year. Rather than spending tens of thousands of dollars hauling in rock to firm up the ground, we usually walk from our cars to the trailer, or drive an ATV to haul supplies if the weather is dry enough to allow passage. Although our access can be a bit of a headache at times, it also reminds us not to buy too much stuff, and the walk home clears our minds and immerses us back into the farm's beauty after a trip to town. We never get door-to-door salesmen or Jehovah's Witnesses, and we're confident that anyone who braves our moat really wants to see us. Overall, my husband and I agree that this inconvenience is a benefit, and not just because it knocked several thousand dollars off the land's asking price.

Right-of-way. This is really a subset of the problematic access point above, but refers to a specific situation in which the property you buy has no road frontage but comes with permission to drive across a neighbor's land to reach your own. Our property has this issue as well, and it caused some problems in the beginning when the neighbor in question wasn't sure about these strangers moving in on the other side of his hayfield. If you ensure that the right-of-way is well documented in the deed (preferably with a map and with the width listed) and then act like a good neighbor, then a right-of-way can become only a minor inconvenience in time.

Unofficial neighborhood codes. You probably won't find many official neighborhood covenants out in rural areas, but you are likely to get pressure from your neighbors to conform to their standards if everyone else has a perfectly manicured lawn. At the other extreme, certain subsets of back-to-the-landers might be annoyed every time they drive home if the neighborhood code runs toward the opposite extreme, with junked cars in the front yard and grass above your head. Personally, I prefer the latter scenario since it means I'm able to try whatever crazy permaculture notion flits through my mind (and since property taxes are considerably lower in that type of area), but to many homesteaders, trashy yards in the neighborhood would be a sign of an ugly-duckling property. On the other hand, if you're interested in green building techniques or want to install a composting toilet, keep in mind that the more manicured neighborhoods are also much more likely to adhere strictly to local building codes and to expect you to do the same.

Run-down farmland. A well-managed farm, with good fences, solidly-vegetated pastures, and rich garden soil is bound to have a higher asking price than the farm that has been abandoned for decades and has reverted to briars. As a new homesteader, though, I think you're better off with the latter, not only to save money, but also to rein in your enthusiasm to manageable levels. Despite having 58 acres to play with, eight years into our homesteading adventure, we currently farm less than two acres and that keeps us plenty busy. Brush can be cleared away and organic matter can be added back to eroded soil, but if you step into ten acres of paradise, you won't have time to do anything except keep the pastures open and the vineyard clear of weeds. Traditionally managed properties are also much more likely to be full of pesticide and herbicide residue than their neglected counterparts. So, once again, price isn't the only reason to choose the ugly-duckling property.

Utilities. Farms that have water, sewer, phone, Internet, and electric ready for hookup are going to cost much more than those with none of the above. On the other hand, depending on how carefully you adhere to building codes, you may spend as much or more on developing systems of your own if utilities aren't already in place. See the "Basic facilities" section at the end of this chapter for more information.

Wealth of the region. The obvious way to find an ugly-duckling property is to look for economically depressed parts of the country (or world). Visit www.cdc.gov/pcd/issues/2007/oct/07_0091. htm to see a breakdown of poverty levels within the United States by county. Here in Appalachia, my problematic land went for $600 per acre in 2003, and similarly cheap farms are still available. As usual, there's a trade-off—poor areas have no high-paying jobs within driving distance, and it's hard to create a local business because most of your neighbors live below the poverty line. However, if you're willing to leverage the power of the Internet to peddle your wares to a wealthier audience elsewhere, you can make a good living no matter where you're located, bringing much-needed dollars into the local economy in the process. (See my ebook *Microbusiness Independence* for more information.) One final caveat: it may not be worth moving all the way across the country to find cheap land if all the people you care about will be more than a day's drive away; homesteading works best with a strong support network.

Proximity to town. The closer you are to a town, especially one with a larger, wealthier population, the more your land will cost per acre. Even if jobs aren't an issue, you're going to have to decide whether you're willing to drive an hour and a half to the big city when you want to find fancier grocery items or to reach a movie theater, library, bar, music establishment, or other entertainment venue of your choice. Finally, distance from a city becomes even trickier if you don't have a romantic partner because the rural dating scene can be dicey. On the other hand, sociable people living in a woodland paradise often find innovative ways to tempt their friends into coming to them, and you may find that you don't miss big-city entertainment options when your own daily life is more fulfilling.

Lay of the land. In addition to creating access issues, the landscape of your farm can affect your ability to catch the sun's rays with solar panels or passive-solar, it will determine whether you have plentiful water for irrigation, and it will impact how easy it is to grade a flat home site. You might also need to consider wind, frost pockets, invasive plants, and whether the mineral rights to your property are owned by someone else. These are characteristics that I recommend not compromising on if you can help it—our north-facing aspect causes problems that are much harder to fix than eroded soil, while, on the other hand, our copious supply of water greatly simplifies gardening.

This is a far-from-comprehensive list, but I hope it gets you thinking about which ugly-duckling features you are and aren't willing to put up with. When I was searching for land, my uncompromising points were that I wanted a large creek and lots of acres without problematic invasive species, so I put up with a long drive to the nearest city, an economically depressed region, and our problematic access. Eleven years later, our ugly-duckling property has turned out to be nearly perfect, and as a bonus, property taxes come in right around $25 per month. Now that's a housing cost we can afford!

Moving and installing a trailer

Trailer-hauling companies possess the proper equipment and will be aware of local regulations pertaining to moving your trailer.

Unless you own a tractor trailer, moving your mobile home to its new location is one of the few tasks that you will definitely want to outsource to the experts. As I mentioned in an earlier chapter, the distance you have to move your trailer will determine how much this endeavor costs—expect to spend at least $200 per hour paying a trailer-moving company to get your new home into place. The good news is that these companies are quite adept at maneuvering mobile homes into the most remote locations, whether that's on top of a mountain or across a river, so they'll soon pay for themselves if your new home will be located on an ugly-duckling property.

Assuming you're buying (or being given) an old, ramshackle trailer, you can save some cash by preparing the structure to be moved yourself. Remove any skirting from around the base (and take the materials with you—they might be reusable); unhook electric, gas, and water lines; and secure furniture and doors so they won't shift or break during travel. If your trailer is as decrepit as ours was, use two-by-fours to form an X over window or door openings, which will prevent the frame of the trailer from distorting as the structure rolls over uneven ground. Finally, make sure the axles and wheels are still attached (if not, you'll need to rent some), then pump up the tires and replace any that don't hold air.

If you're moving into a remote location, your crew will probably transfer the mobile home from a tractor trailer to a bulldozer once they leave the road.

With the exception of travel trailers, mobile homes are too large to be pulled behind even a hefty pickup truck, so after preparing for the move, you'll need to leave the next part to the pros and their tractor trailer. Your trailer-hauling service should be on top of any local permitting and insurance issues, along with requirements for including "wide load" signage and warning vehicles in your entourage.

This is also the time to decide whether you want to pay extra to have the new house site graded. Although it's relatively easy for your movers to jack the trailer up so it's level on uneven ground, your trailer may last longer if they use a bulldozer to create a flat, raised pad so that water drains away from the trailer on every side.

Tie-downs can be a DIY project, but check local building codes.

Installation should probably also be left to the pros since they need large jacks to get the trailer up onto cinder-block piers. You'll need to purchase tie-downs, which are simply long metal screws that you twist into the ground and attach to your trailer with metal straps to prevent the wind from blowing your home away. Within hours, your trailer could be ready to move into!

Basic facilities

If you're moving into a well-populated area such as a trailer park or suburb, chances are you'll be required to hook into existing utility lines, including sewer, water, and electricity. But if you're trailersteading back in the boondocks, some or all of these facilities will be left up to your discretion. Assuming you're willing to skimp and build things yourself, you might end up with a more environmentally friendly system for a fraction of the cost.

For example, most areas require a health-department-approved septic system before you can connect to the electric grid. But if you want to do without electricity or already have electricity on the property, chances are the authorities will ignore your composting toilet until and unless they get complaints from your neighbors. Similarly, if there's an outhouse on your property already, this alternative method of sewage management may be grandfathered in. Of course, I'm not advocating straight pipes or outhouses that negatively impact the groundwater. Instead, flip to the sections "Experiments with humanure" and "Greywater wetland" if you'd like to learn how my husband and I built cheap, effective, and environmentally friendly treatment systems for our homestead's waste.

If you have a source of chemical-free and moderately clean water, a sediment filter and UV light may be all you need to filter your drinking water. Even without treatment, the original water can be used for washing.

What about water? The conventional method of tapping into a water source if you live beyond the reach of city water lines is to drill a well, but that process can cost thousands of dollars. On the other hand, if you don't have to jump through health-department hoops (for the reasons outlined in the previous paragraph), a shallow hand-dug well or boxed-in spring might be a better choice for your trailerstead. Both of these types of low-tech water systems typically contain small amounts of coliform bacteria and moderate amounts of sediment, but you can treat this mostly-clean water quite easily with a low-cost sediment-filter-and-ultraviolet-light combination. If you really want to trailerstead on the cheap, you can also repeat our early adventure of carrying drinking water home from public springs and friends' houses—we learned in the process that we only truly need about a gallon of water per person per day for drinking and rinsing off fresh produce, making the transport of potable water only moderately arduous.

Although I'm a fan of building your own sewage and water systems, I'm less keen on homegrown electricity since small-scale green-energy solutions tend to cost more money than they save. It can definitely feel satisfying to live off the grid with the help of your own solar panels, hydropower, or windmill, but you might be better off financially if you stay connected. The exception, once again, is do-it-yourself systems, especially those cobbled together out of used parts. See the profile "An incognito trailer" for one example of a home-made, off-grid energy system that definitely makes financial sense.

All of these choices aside, you might as well allot the cash to hook your trailer up conventionally if you're the type of person who's going to lie awake at night and wait for the authorities to discover your sidesteps of the law. Unfortunately, developing basic facilities that are up to code can be even more expensive than moving your trailer into place. For example, Sara and Seth (profiled in the next section) spent $6,000 installing a septic tank and well, and we paid our electric company nearly $1,300 for power hookup despite erecting our own pole and wiring our own box rather than paying an electrician. Even with these figures included, though, installing a trailer is drastically cheaper than building or buying a similarly sized house.

Case study: Starter home for a young family
Farming from a trailer

"I've wanted to be a farmer for most of my life...Living on this property has given me lots of learning opportunities."

Photo credit: Sara and Seth McDonald

Sara McDonald lives in a mobile home in southeast Louisiana with her husband Seth, two children, a dog, and a cat. Sara's mother gave them a place to stay in Virginia for about a year after their first child was born, but Seth and Sara soon chose to move down to vacant land in Louisiana that was in Seth's family.

A trailer was a shortcut to moving onto a piece of vacant land owned by her husband's family, where Sara now has room to experiment.

Photo credit: Sara and Seth McDonald

"I never wanted to work a full-time job away from home," explained Sara. "I've wanted to be a farmer most of my life, and while I wouldn't classify myself as a farmer today, living on this property has given me a lot of learning opportunities. I've spent a lot of time foraging for mushrooms and wild plants, planting new trees in the pastures, and starting a small orchard. This is possible because of where we live, but also because I don't feel like I have to work at a day job all day just to survive. I actually quit my job recently, reducing our income by over 50 percent. Since we've paid off the loans to buy and set up the trailer, I wasn't nearly as stressed out about leaving my job as I might have been otherwise. I feel like I'm incredibly fortunate."

Family reaction to the trailer life

Sara reports that trailers are considered acceptable starter homes for young families in her area.

Photo credit: Sara and Seth McDonald

Sara and Seth were lucky to have the support of most of their family when it came time to make housing decisions. An old farmhouse stood on the land they ultimately moved onto but "there was a lot of opposition to our insistence on moving back into the old house. Ultimately, if we wanted to live on the family property, we would have to build a new house or move into a trailer. That pretty much decided it for us. We didn't want to spend the time and money to build a house right away. I was also hesitant to spend a lot of money on new building materials. It seems like a waste when there are so many decent dwellings sitting around empty. A recycled dwelling seemed like a good idea. It's more consistent with my values, and it was cost-effective."

Seth's family and Sara's father had plenty of experience with trailers. "Seth lived in a trailer most of his life, and his mom was really supportive of our decision," Sara said, going on to note that Seth's mother had recently sold her trailer for $3,000 more than she'd invested in it "casting some doubt on the common belief that trailers always depreciate." Sara's father came from the mountains of Virginia where "most of my younger cousins who are just starting out consider themselves lucky if they have a trailer to live in, even living in trailer parks." Even though Sara herself had grown up in apartments, her mother had "always yearned for ownership, so she was happy that we'd actually own something and be on our own property."

"I think people in the South have negative biases against trailers, but they also tend to accept them as an option for people in certain life stages," Sara explained. "Being a young family in a rural area or small town, a trailer is a fairly acceptable 'starter home.' I think retirees are also afforded some leniency when it comes to trailer stereotypes.

"Seth's dad is the only one who really seems kind of uneasy with the idea of us living in a trailer long-term." Sara seemed to find this small amount of resistance amusing, noting that her father-in-law is also the only one of their parents who currently lives in a travel trailer. "He always tells us we need a real house, and that we shouldn't have to live in this thing forever. Of course, he's the one who found it for us, but I think he was just eager to have us move back to Louisiana."

Trailer concerns

Photo credit: Sara and Seth McDonald

Keeping her children safe from fires tops Sara's list of concerns about living in a mobile home.

Although Sara's analysis of her living arrangement was very positive overall, she did have some major concerns. Foremost was fire, which she explains is "one reason my son sleeps in the bedroom with my husband and me. He has his own little bed in our room, and it's because I don't want to even risk being separated from him by fire. The furnace is between our bedroom and the second bedroom so it just seems too risky to me."

Due to their hurricane-prone location, she also worries about the mobile home being blown away. "Our trailer went through Katrina, Rita, Gustav, and most recently Isaac, without any issues at all. It gives me some sense of security for our belongings, but I still would not want to stay in it during a big storm." She's considering erecting "some kind of small wind shelter" to give the family a place to retreat to during high winds. "I've looked at FEMA safe-building plans that were priced at around $7,500 for wood with steel reinforcement, and about $11,000 to $13,000 for concrete and steel buildings that are 8x14. We are also considering a sturdy port-like structure over the trailer since we will need to replace our roof soon, and I'd like to design it in a way that strengthens the whole building against wind. So far, I have found conflicting research on this, and some of the research shows that modifications can make the building more vulnerable to wind damage, so I'm holding off for now."

Photo credit: Sara and Seth McDonald

"Most of my attempts to reduce energy costs come in the form of strategic plantings around the house," said Sara. "Our trees are finally growing tall enough to provide a decent amount of shade to the southern and western walls in the summer."

Since Sara is environmentally conscious, she also dislikes the amount of energy required to heat and cool their home. She and her husband spend an average of $70 per month on energy, which includes both electric heating and cooling. On the other hand, she notes that "the apartment I lived in [before moving into the trailer] was maybe $30 less a month during the middle of the summer, and about the same during fall and spring. That's maybe a total of $200 a year more that we spend in the trailer, but it is well offset by the lack of other bills and payments we have to make."

Inexpensive living

Living in a trailer has recently given Sara the opportunity to be a stay-at-home mom.

The biggest advantage of living in a mobile home for Sara's family has been the low housing costs. "We paid $15,500 with a five-year loan, about 4.5 percent interest, which turned out to be payments of about $280 a month. A couple years earlier, I was paying the same amount for my share of the rent in an apartment that I shared with a roommate, so it was nice that I'd actually own something at the end of five years," Sara said, putting the cost in perspective.

In addition to the price of the trailer, Sara and Seth spent another $6,000 to improve the property and prepare for the trailer with a septic tank and well, then a final $1,000 to have the trailer delivered and installed. Now that the loan and setup costs are paid off, though, the family is able to live on less than $1,000 per month "and that includes student-loan debt and emergency health insurance."

"If we had to build a house here, we probably couldn't afford it for at least another twenty years unless we wanted to go into serious debt," Sara noted. "The trailer has definitely made it possible for us to live in a nice location on a fairly large property (twenty acres).

"The mobile part of the 'mobile home' is also a nice perk. We own one acre, but since the rest of the land around us is family land and will eventually be subdivided and possibly sold, we may want to move somewhere else in the future. Being able to pack up our home and take it with us is a comforting notion (though I won't be able to take my gardens!).

"On a philosophical note, I really sympathize with people who are having trouble finding decent housing during the current economic crisis. I think it's a shame that our society so eagerly embraced expensive housing on the premise that house values appreciate indefinitely and you'll always get some return on your investment. What a waste. That part of the 'American Dream' has driven so many people to financial ruin and it has made housing so unaffordable that people can scarcely even consider owning a home before they are at least five years into a steady career—and then only when they are willing to take on the major debt of a mortgage. To actually own a traditional home outright (especially a new construction) seems like a distant dream that will never come true for a lot of people."

To read more about Sara's adventures, visit her blog at www.wildhomestead. org. Her ebooks include *A 10-Acre Permaculture Project* and *One Acre Homestead*, both of which are available on Amazon.

REMODELING
A TRAILER

Trailer overhauls

In the summer of 2012, Mark and I discovered a local carpenter who has remodeled and overhauled dozens of mobile homes over the last decade (as well as building and fixing up an equal number of traditional houses). I sat down with Bradley and asked him about the most common ailments of the mobile home.

"A trailer ain't worth a dime," Bradley declared. Although he lives in a mobile home himself, the builder considers the structures to be under-built and dangerous, with walls constructed from two-by-twos (instead of two-by-fours) and with far too many electrical outlets per breaker. "They're built in a hurry for mass production," he explained, "and nothing is level or built out of real wood."

A leaky roof caused plenty of problems early in our trailer adventure. Here, Mark is replacing wet insulation after sealing a crack between sheets of roofing metal.

"So how do people make a trailer more livable?" I asked.

Bradley noted that the first thing many mobile-home dwellers want updated is the roof. (See "Adding a pitched roof to a mobile home" for more information on our own endeavor.) Then Bradley typically takes off the siding and reframes the walls with two-by-fours or two-by-sixes to create a larger cavity for additional wall insulation. Afterward, the siding can be screwed back in place, or you can upgrade to house-style vinyl siding. A later section suggests a few other alternatives for increasing the insulative value of trailer walls.

Insulation under the floor often needs to be replaced next. Bradley explained that the old insulation is usually held in place by black netting (although in our 1960s-era trailer, there was instead a type of particleboard holding the insulation up against the underside of the floor). Bradley removes and throws away the netting, pushes R19 insulation up between the floor joists, and then adds a synthetic underlayment, which is a breathable fiberglass-embedded fabric.

The next step is flooring, in which category older trailers actually fare better than newer models. After about 1988, mobile-home manufacturers began building with pressed sawdust board that eventually rots through, meaning that this type of floor often needs to be re-studded around the sinks and toilet, then the particleboard is replaced with a water-resistant OSB board. Advantech is Bradley's preferred brand for flooring since it's rated to sit out in the weather for at least six months without breaking down and comes with a 40-year warranty under regular use.

"What's the next most common request?" I asked.

"Windows and doors," Bradley replied, explaining that the single-glazed windows that come standard in trailers leak cold air in the winter. "Then cabinets and general interior remodeling. After about ten or fifteen years, you basically have to rebuild a trailer one room at a time." The builder explained that vents start to leak and that electrical wiring and plumbing need to be repaired or replaced as a trailer ages. In addition, the roof may let rain through if you don't mop on a sealer every three to five years (assuming you didn't top your trailer with a new roof).

Then there are the underpinnings (or skirting). Since a trailer is basically a house on wheels, most homeowners opt to close in the area between the outside walls and the ground for the sake of insulation and aesthetics. Adding a skirt of solid material around the bottom of the mobile home keeps cold air from blowing right under your trailer in the winter (which means the floor is warmer and your heating bill is lower), and skirting generally makes a mobile home fit in better within a more upscale neighborhood.

Although many trailer-dwellers have been choosing vinyl siding recently during their skirting projects, Bradley notes that the materials only last about three years. His favorite underpinning is galvanized, which can stand up to about 30 to 40 years of weather (although the galvanized skirting might need a coat of paint after about a decade). In our area in 2012, galvanized underpinnings cost about $7 for a 3-foot-by-5-foot sheet. Alternatively, you might want to consider the low-cost alternatives in the section "DIY insulated skirting" if you're willing to expend a bit more effort for the sake of warmer floors.

A more expensive option is to skip the skirting and to put your trailer up on a real cinder-block foundation. This is a much more permanent solution, so you won't want to spend the money if there's a chance you might want to move your trailer someday, but the cinder blocks do help support the trailer and prevent bowing of the floor over time. Rebecca (profiled in the case study "Hiding in the vegetation") reported that her husband built a foundation beneath their single-wide with small bump-out for under $1,000, although she admits that he "used quite a bit of materials he had on hand" and that "the cost of concrete has doubled since then." As you'll see in the next case study, David's full basement came in around $9,000.

Although all of this information may make you wonder why you'd live in a structure that needs so much attention, free or cheap trailers can save you a lot of money since you're able to remodel slowly over time rather than falling deeply into debt by purchasing a house. As Mark and I have discovered, a trailer is extremely forgiving of know-nothing DIYers, and it feels a bit like building with Legos to unscrew the siding, frame up a wall of double-glazed windows, and suddenly have a completely new living space. So keep reading for tips on cheap and easy ways to turn your trailer into a comfortable home, and remember that most aspects of trailer remodeling are as easy—or easier—than similar remodels in a stick-built home.

DIY insulated skirting

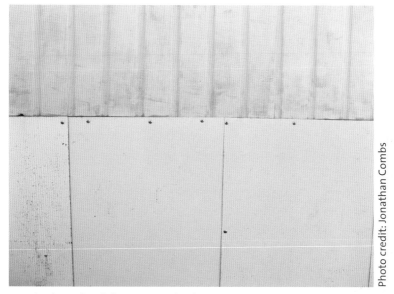

Photo credit: Jonathan Combs

Jonathan's insulated skirting is made of pieces cut out of door panels.

Jonathan, profiled in the case study "Trailer park to woodland paradise," found an ingenious, cheap, and energy-efficient solution to skirting his trailer. "The panels we used are waste products from the manufacture of exterior doors," he explained. "The solid doors are constructed first, then an opening is cut out for any glass that will be installed, leaving a rectangular piece of unused material.

"There is a location near us that sells these panels. The panels we used are approximately 20 inches by 36 inches and consist of a foam center covered with painted aluminum or fiberglass on the front and back. We cut them to the desired length, dug a shallow trench for the bottom of the panel to sit in, then screwed them in place and raked dirt back up around the bottom, both inside and out, to hold the bottom in place."

Jonathan noted that the materials used to skirt his 14-by-70-foot single-wide cost $325, which is similar to the price of vinyl skirting. "I believe this has had a significant impact on heating and cooling," he noted.

In addition to insulation and flashing, you'll need a few basic tools to create your own insulated skirting. We used a hand saw, marker, tape measurer, and straight edge. (No, a utility knife doesn't do the job very well, nor does a bread knife make the cut.)

While Mark and I would have loved to follow Jonathan's lead, we weren't able to find a similar door-manufacturing plant near us. Instead, we came up with an off-the-shelf solution, cutting sheets of inch-thick rigid-foam insulation using a hand saw, then fitting the pieces into the gap between the walls of our trailer and the ground.

With the help of a scrap of wood . . .

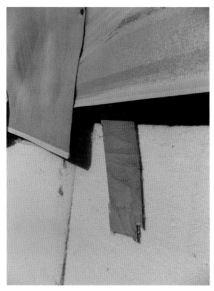

... the insulation sheets slid into place without any special attachment.

Although I'd originally planned to install wooden rails along the ground as an attachment point for the bottom edge of our insulated sheets, I instead found that the insulation was easy to wedge up under the trailer's siding, staying in place with the help of a simple scrap of eighth-inch-thick wood.

A layer of metal flashing on the outside of the insulated sheets protects the foam from weather and marauding chickens. At the right side of this photo, you can see the drainage pipe that I put into place before installing the siding in order to channel water from the gutters to the other side of the trailer, where it eventually flows into our greywater wetland.

Next, I added a sheet of galvanized flashing (similarly tucked up under the trailer's siding) to protect the insulation from weather (and from free-range chickens, who love pecking Styrofoam to bits). Finally, I mounded up earth about eight inches deep on the outside of the skirting to form a flower bed along the side of our trailer, and to hold the bottom of the skirting in place. The result wasn't elegant, but once I planted an array of easy flowers in front (see the section "Shade trellis to cool your home with plants"), we had a fast, easy, and functional skirting solution.

We only installed ten feet of this skirting the first year since we wanted to ensure that the simple solution would go the distance. But now that the experimental section has survived a year of weathering while also improving our trailer's aesthetics, we're busy finishing the other 110 linear feet. I have high hopes that fully enclosing the area under our trailer will serve to decrease our heating expenses in the future, just as Jonathan's insulated skirting helped his home stay warm during the winter months.

Case study: An incognito trailer
Hidden in plain sight

Photo credit: David and Mary

David and Mary's beautiful home is built around a 1974 trailer.

"I almost never tell anyone that we live in a trailer because, with a normal gable roof and a full basement, we both consider it a normal stick-built house," David said. "Although if a visitor happens to mention that we have a very nice place, I will then tell them it was at one time a 'mobile home' now converted to real estate."

Mary and David in 1993. David said, "I basically look the same now, just less hair."

Photo credit: PharMor

Over the past three decades, Mary and David have created a vibrant homestead, due in part to the low cost of their initial housing choice. What I enjoyed most about David's story is that he and his wife both worked blue-collar jobs, but they didn't have to wait until they struck it rich or retired to start homesteading. You may find the in-depth information on renovating a mobile home equally inspiring.

Pulling themselves up by their bootstraps

David and Mary in 1974.

Photo credit: Louis Fortunato

Mary and David met in 1973 at a Beach Boy concert in Youngstown, Ohio. "I worked in a steel-processing plant as an industrial electrician, while Mary worked at an aluminum-extrusion plant in office accounting," David said.

The pair saved their pennies and bought a 1974 14-by-60-foot mobile home for $5,000 soon after getting married in 1979. But "life was not very good in a mobile-home park. Kids yelling, doors banging, engines revving, lawn mowers without mufflers, and the neighbors thought we were standoffish when we were just working a regular job and coming home tired after a hard day at work," David remembered.

The couple dreamed of buying a piece of land in the country, and two years later they made that dream a reality when they found seven acres of wooded land within their price range. Unfortunately, some stormy waters were ahead. "This was 1981," David said. "Inflation was running wild, prime interest rates were 18 percent to 20 percent. Big time recession, and after signing a three-year land contract and moving our house to the property, our union went on strike.

"With so many people out of work because of the recession, I just couldn't find a job anywhere unless we were willing to move out of the area, which some people call the 'rust belt' because of the steel mills closing in 1975. Moving from the area was not an option—Mary was still employed with her company—so we would just have to watch our money closely and make do with less."

As you'll see, David and Mary made do very well, turning their trailer into a modern home a bit at a time as they could afford the expenditures. Now David feels lucky to live where he does. "We have our savings and investments, produce most of our own power, produce some of our own food, and we owe no man nothing." What better argument could be made for trailersteading?

Turning a trailer into a home

David and Mary had a lot of work ahead of them before they could rest on their laurels, and they were well aware of the disadvantages of the cheap-housing option. "The construction of our mobile home was typical for the time period, corrugated aluminum siding, metal roof, marginal wall insulation because it was less than two-by-four stud construction, paneling for inside walls, single-pane windows that leaked air like a sieve (and froze over in the winter), cardboard doors (no joke), hollow plastic doors on kitchen cabinets (which held up extremely well over the years), shag carpeting, chrome-plated plastic faucets, and what looked like a 15-to-20-gallon hot-water tank. (We ran out of hot water a lot.) I will say this, even though everything was cheap construction, for the most part everything was in good condition, neat, clean, and organized, and that is the way we kept it for a long time."

David working on his mobile home in its new location.

Photo credit: David and Mary

With the help of family, neighbors, and contractors, David and Mary began improving their trailer when they could afford each step. The land they moved to had a septic tank and "something that resembled a driveway," but the couple spent $350 to hire a bulldozer and to pay the neighbor and his son to get their mobile home placed on foundation blocks that David had already erected. Later, David installed the electrical entrance cable, used a rented backhoe to attach the trailer to the septic tank, and performed the plumbing himself, but he had to hire a well driller and gravel truck to provide water and access to the land.

Photo credit: David and Mary

Their first major improvement was to contract out a pitched roof added onto their mobile home.

At this point, David was back at work, and by 1985, he and Mary had saved enough to hire a cousin to add a roof onto their trailer and to pour loose insulation into the attic.

Building a full basement cost $9,000 in 1985 or 1986.

Photo credit: David and Mary

First, the couple constructed the basement out of cinder blocks.

Photo credit: David and Mary

Then they slid the mobile home on top using I beams.

Photo credit: David and Mary

A year or two later, the couple built a basement below the trailer, then hired a contractor to install double-glazed windows and redwood siding.

Hunting around until they found a good deal on cheap insulation made it possible to upgrade the energy efficiency of their home. These unfaced fiberglass rolls of insulation were manufacturer surplus at $20 per roll, and the one-inch-thick rigid foam boards cost $3 to $9 per sheet "depending on defects."

"We loved the looks of the siding, but it needed constant maintenance with oil wood preservative," David remembered. Meanwhile "the wood-boring bees loved to get behind the aluminum gutters and bore holes into the fascia boards. I wasn't going to let some insect destroy our home. We also wanted more insulation in the walls, and the only way to accomplish that was to put the insulation on the outside."

Removing the siding exposes the insulation.

The trailer itself had about three inches of fiberglass insulation in the walls, to which David added foil-faced foam boards for extra heat-holding power. He "taped all the seams with aluminum tape and used special nails to hold the foam board in place."

Photo credit: David and Mary

Adding rigid insulation to the outside of the wall is an easy way to increase thermal efficiency.

About the same time, Mary and David hired a contractor to install aluminum fascia under the gutters and on the rakes of the roof, along with vinyl perforated soffit to protect the attic insulation from moisture.

Photo credit: David and Mary

The redwood siding was beautiful, but labor-intensive.

"As you can see from these photos, we have come a long way since the original metal-sided, metal-roof trailer that we had before," David said. "You can also see a well-insulated house, but no siding, a large deck, but no railing, no lattice, and most of the decking isn't fastened down."

David and Mary's home continued to improve over time.

Photo credit: David and Mary

As with most homesteads, David and Mary's is still a work in progress. When not improving their home, David keeps busy building an "Amish-style laundry line from BMX bike wheels and stainless-steel wire rope," installing an orchard, digging an irrigation pond, and fencing out deer.

"There are also the small jobs like trimming trees, mowing grass, working on our car and truck, canning thirty pounds of chicken breast, canning green beans. I think you get the idea."

Alternative energy

David and Mary's homestead in 2010. The glass room was a display model purchased on Ebay for $7,000.

Photo credit: David and Mary

Every homesteader has a pet project—the real reason they want to live on the land—and David's is clearly alternative energy. He converted their heat source from natural gas to propane and then to wood, focused on insulation to minimize already-lowered heating costs, and then moved on to producing electricity.

David's first attempt at getting off the grid was a DIY windmill.

Photo credit: David and Mary

"I wanted to start generating my own power," David wrote. "Photovoltaic panels were too expensive so I decided to build a wind turbine. I bought a tower and batteries from a scrap yard, gearbox, generator, and most of the other parts and components from the local surplus stores in the area, the propeller hub came from an old DC3 plane, and the blades came out of a cooling tower of a steam generating plant. We didn't have a basement at the time so I bought an old travel trailer and gutted everything out to make room for all of the batteries and power-conversion equipment.

"The turbine worked in a fashion. I had no way to control the speed other than loading the generator or turning the brake on, so the use was limited to when we were home, lower wind speeds, or the amount of power we used (very little load if batteries were full). For the most part, my ambitious project just didn't work out, but I kept modifying things trying to make it work."

David's batteries soon made the move to the new basement.

By now, the basement was in place, which gave David a location to store his batteries in a more controlled environment. He also decided to branch out into solar panels, especially since he'd found 3-kilowatts' worth for a low price. "They came from a demonstration solar-power plant in the south California desert. After being cooked in the sun with concentrating mirrors, they were dumped onto the surplus market. I installed them in 1994. I don't remember the cost, but it was cheap at the time."

Two rounds of solar panels lowered their electric bill.

In 2011, more solar panels were added to the roof, this time a 1.6-kilowatt array sold as seconds by www.sunelec.com.

The solar panels from the other side.

When asked about prices, David was vague—he didn't keep track, but knows he got a good deal. "Almost everything we buy, build, and install, is seconds," David explained. "We live in the world of surplus."

Putting the money into a house instead

Today, the trailer is hidden inside David and Mary's modern home.

Many people argue that it doesn't make sense to put large amounts of cash into a mobile home. If you're going to spend that kind of money, why not simply build or buy a stick-built house that is high quality from the get-go? I put this devil's advocate question to each of the folks we interviewed, and I found David's answer to be the most thought-provoking.

David's energy-star appliances upgraded the efficiency of his kitchen.

"If we had bought a big fancy house with a big mortgage instead of the trailer, we probably would have lost it back to the bank because, two weeks after moving the trailer to our new property, I lost my job and was out of work for two years because of the bad economy," David said. "So living in a pre-made structure with wood heat and land contract was cheap living again.

"So let's say after two years I get back to work and money is flowing again, so we decide to build, or contract out the construction of a new house while we lived in the trailer. Would the house be what we wanted, or would it be what we thought we wanted? Would it be two-by-six or two-by-four walls, would the house be too small or too large, would the house be facing south or would we have made the mistake and faced it the wrong direction, would the interior be laid out in a logical manner or would we have followed the contractor/architect's advice and regretted the decision for the rest of our lives?

"If I were to build a house now, I know exactly what I want in a house. I know the type, quality, and placement of windows; I know the thickness of the walls and insulation type; I know the orientation of the structure and placement on the property; I know the roof material; I know on what side of the house utility and low-use rooms should be placed. These are things I didn't know back thirty years ago.

"The mobile homes now are much better quality than our 1974 vintage trailer. Young people (or old people) now can buy a mobile home with two-by-six walls and a regular shingled gabled roof, and vinyl siding. I say if a person can find a good quality used mobile home and move it out to their property, that would save them money, time, and effort. Then they can direct their efforts toward something more productive, like a more self-sustainable lifestyle."

Insulating trailer walls

We learned the basics of mainstream construction techniques when we built an eight-by-twenty-foot structure off the east side of our trailer. This photo shows a wall panel being built atop the floor.

Note how the width of the two-by-fours determines the depth of the wall cavity once the wall framing is stood up into place.

Trailers are built to be light enough to move easily, which means that the walls in many are framed using two-by-twos instead of two-by-four lumber. For those of you who haven't spent any time constructing or remodeling houses, this distinction simply refers to the dimensions of the wood used to frame up (provide the skeleton for) the structure. If you look at a piece of lumber from one end, a two-by-four is two inches on one side and four inches on the other, while a two-by-two is a square that measures two inches on each side. (Well, lumber suppliers actually skimp a bit and shave a quarter of an inch off each side, so a two-by-four really measures 1.75 inches by 3.75 inches. But I'm going to keep this description simple and ignore those fractional inches.)

When framing a house with two-by-fours, the lumber is arranged so that the four-inch width of the board forms the depth of the wall cavity. This cavity is where insulation goes, so a house framed with two-by-fours can accommodate 3.75-inch-thick, R13 insulation. (See

Our trailer was originally designed to have a bay window at one end, but the glass had been removed by the time we purchased the dwelling. Since the replacement windows we had on hand were a different size than the originals, Mark tore out the entire area, reframed it with two-by-four lumber, and created a slightly larger (if not-quite-symmetrical) bay.

the section "Adding a pitched roof to a mobile home" for more information on R-values, but for now, you just need to understand that bigger R-values mean more insulation, which means your house stays cooler in the summer and warmer in the winter.) R13 insulation just happens to be the recommended value for walls in most parts of the United States, which is one of the reasons that many of us build our homes out of two-by-fours in the first place.

In contrast, a trailer built with two-by-two lumber can accommodate only half that thickness of insulation, which means that the typical trailersteader is only getting half as much heat-retention power in his walls as the government recommends. While Mark and I have reframed areas beneath replacement windows with two-by-four lumber in order to accommodate thicker insulation, tearing out all of the walls in an existing trailer just to add insulation usually doesn't make sense. Is there a better solution for increasing in-wall R-values?

Photo credit: David and Mary

Adding rigid insulation to the outside of a trailer is one way to work around the low R-value provided by two-by-two framing.

David (profiled in "An incognito trailer") would answer that question with an unequivocal "Yes!" He took advantage of a siding upgrade to improve his wall-insulation problem by adding two layers of inch-thick rigid-foam-board (polyisocyanurate) insulation to the outside of his trailer. After coating the rigid insulation with half-inch sheets of plywood, his walls had been upgraded to a final insulation value of R26, or twice the government recommendation. Since David scrounged for supplies and found them on sale, he was able to re-insulate the walls, upgrade the ceiling insulation from R19 to R60, and add insulation to the basement, all for about $500.

Are there even more outside-the-box solutions to the trailer-wall-insulation problem? Some alternative-building techniques like cob and straw bales have potential for increasing the thickness and insulative power of your walls, but these techniques will require a bit more effort (and an extended roof overhang in most cases). Alternatively, you can work with the walls you already have, adding a framework along the north face of your trailer to grow an evergreen creeper like English ivy for winter insulation, while shading the south and west sides with deciduous plants. The chapter "Heating and cooling a mobile home" includes other options for working with the sun and with plants to lower your winter-heating costs.

Interior renovations

If I showed you a photo of the interior of Mark's and my trailer, most of you would close this book in disgust. The truth is that I'm not very interested in aesthetics, so my husband and I have done very little to

Photo credit: David and Mary

The inside of David and Mary's house is indistinguishable from any other modern American home.

improve the interior of our trailer beyond the basics required for safe and cozy living. However, I know that many potential trailersteaders are held back by their inability to envision living inside a decrepit mobile home, so I thought I'd include a short section with a few tips on interior renovation done trailer style.

Although Mark and I have little experience with the topic, David and Mary (profiled in the section "An incognito trailer") could write a whole book on the subject. In addition to the extensive work that the couple have put into upgrading their home's external appearance and functionality, they've also improved the interior until their trailer is nearly indistinguishable from any other modern house.

I was particularly taken with David's ingenious use of in-wall storage, such as this door that opens to let down an ironing board. In another example of trailersteader ingenuity, the pulley beside the ironing board attaches to a weight that is used to keep the top of the bedroom door open at night while the bottom half stays closed, ensuring that heat but no cats enter the couple's bedroom while humans are sleeping.

Photo credit: David and Mary

Like many other trailersteaders, the couple's first step was to rip out the paneling and replace it with drywall. David noted that during his own wall-remodeling project, he was careful to add a vapor barrier (which was originally absent from his walls) and to tape all seams, including around outlets and wall switches. If you're following David's lead, this is also a good time to upgrade the in-wall insulation and to add any new pipes or electrical wiring that you may want in the future. Otherwise, renovating trailer walls is identical to changing out drywall in any other stick-built house.

Photo credit: David and Mary

Another in-wall cabinet holds kitchen appliances.

"Because of limited space," David continued, "almost all of our cabinets are built in with no space behind. This saves room and also adds R-value (insulation) to the walls. The only downfall is there is no changing the location of the furniture in the rooms."

Although beautiful cabinets and wooden trim bring the couple's bedroom to life, David notes that this is the only room in the house where he left the original paneling in place. "I regret not doing it the correct way," he said, "but with several coats of latex paint on the wall, there doesn't seem to be a problem from moisture."

Photo credit: David and Mary

When asked how much his interior renovations cost, David reminded me that most of his supplies were damaged freight and seconds. "Renovation cost?" he said. "I don't have a clue. No loans, everything was out-of-pocket money, so pick a number." However, he did add that the beautiful cabinets featured in their living room and bedroom are from a KraftMaid manufacturer that "dumps their seconds, discontinued, and damaged cabinets and trim work on the surplus market."

For other inspiring images of rehabbed trailer interiors, check out the profiles "Cheap and green" and "A holler full of family." And maybe in the next edition of this book, I'll have some tips of my own to share. After all, I *do* dream of adding a straw-bale shell around the outside of our trailer and installing tile floors in front of our bank of south-facing windows for thermal mass. I'm sure that Mark and I will get around to those improvements . . . after I grow bored with learning to milk goats and with terraforming our swamp, that is.

That said, if making the interior of your trailerstead aesthetically appealing is a bit higher on your own priority list, I hope that David's example will prove that you don't have to cut corners just because you live in a trailer. With some surplus supplies and a lot of elbow grease, your mobile home can make the neighbors just as jealous as David and Mary's does.

Installing a stove hood

A stove hood is a good first step for mobile-home fire prevention.

As I mentioned in the section on fire, adding a hood above your stove circumvents one of the most hazardous features of the average mobile home—flammable cabinets located directly above a cooking surface. This project costs about $100 in supplies plus a few hours of labor, for which price you'll soon enjoy less buildup of grease on nearby surfaces and more peace of mind about the possibility of kitchen fires.

Your first step when embarking on a stove-hood project is to select the type of hood you plan to install. We chose a ducted—rather than a ductless—stove hood, figuring that a slightly more difficult initial installation was a fair exchange for not having to replace filters every month. In addition, ducted hoods have the advantage of flushing smoky air into the outdoors rather than recirculating irritants through the air you're breathing in the kitchen, making a ducted hood the obvious selection for health reasons.

Of course, with a ducted stove hood, you have to create a hole in the wall (the duct) for the smoky air to pass through. This ductwork can be complicated in a large house, especially if your range is placed against an inside wall, but trailers are usually so narrow that the range is generally located along a wall that separates your kitchen from the outdoors. As a result, ductwork in a trailer is relatively simple.

Renovating trailers is easy because wall coverings usually consist of thin sheets of wood or cardboard.

A problematic stud is easy to remove with a reciprocating saw.

Sealing any cracks with silicone will keep cold air out in the winter. In this photo, you'll also notice that a header board has been added to the top of the wall opening in order to transfer the weight of the roof to the studs on either side.

A two-by-six acts as a support for the range hood to screw onto.

When installing a ducted stove hood, the first step is to remove the wall covering behind your range and see what's underneath. In our case, a stud was directly in the way of the planned opening and had to be removed, a simple feat with a reciprocating saw. However, every stud you remove lessens the structural integrity of your trailer, so we firmed up the opening by adding a two-by-four header board across the top of the wall.

While a range hood can be screwed directly onto trailer studs, Mark felt that our two-by-two studs were a bit puny for this application, and the studs also weren't in the precise right location. So we chose to beef up our support structure by running a two-by-four from floor to ceiling on one side. The other side of the hood area butts up against our wood-stove alcove, which we built using two-by-four lumber and thus felt was sound enough to easily hold the weight of the range hood. Finally, we added a modified two-by-six to span the area between these two studs, resulting in a very solid support to attach our hood onto.

A duct wall cap goes through a hole in the exterior siding to attach directly into the back of the range hood.

As you probably noticed in these photos, we cut a rectangular section out of the top of our two-by-six support just the right size for the ductwork in the back of the range hood to fit through. A duct wall cap sliding into a similar hole in the outside of the trailer completes the vent assembly.

As a side note, we considered cobbling together our own covering for the exterior vent opening, but ended up being glad to have splurged $25 on a premade wall cap. The included damper within our cap is perfectly calibrated to open when our hood's fan blows, then to close quickly when the fan stops, separating inside and outside air whenever our stove isn't in use. As a result, this damper prevents warm house air from being lost to the outdoors on winter nights and also stops hot summer air from flowing inside on muggy days.

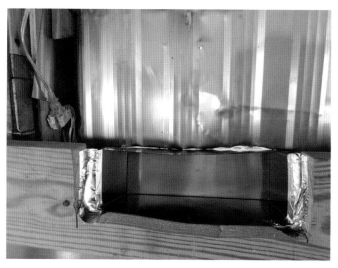

Anywhere you see light should be sealed with tape or silicone.

As Mark worked, he was careful to seal any gaps with reflective tape or silicone. We also upgraded the insulation in this area while the wall was torn apart since the trailer's original insulation was compressed and had lost much of its insulative value. If you need an extra electrical socket, this would also be your chance to modify any wiring in this portion of the wall.

Your range hood will provide instructions for wiring and installation.

I won't go into the specifics of assembling your range hood here since every model will be slightly different, but chances are good that you'll need to wire an electrical plug into your hood to power the fan. In addition, most hoods are made so they can vent either up or out the back, so you may need to move the connecting damper to its proper slot on the back of the range hood. Otherwise, the hood should just slide into the hole you created for it, then screw into place on the support behind.

The finished stove hood is ready to suck pollutants out of the kitchen.

One final piece of advice: If you plan to add a shelf above your range hood or to build cabinets back into this space, be sure to add a piece of cement board or other fireproof barrier between the range hood and any flammable lumber. We're slowly removing all of the cabinets from our trailer to make it easier to keep track of our appliances, so Mark instead faced the new wall area with pegboard for easy attachment.

Once again, a simple DIY project has helped bring our fifty-year-old trailer into the twenty-first century. And maybe now our smoke detectors won't go off every time I fry bacon.

Adding a pitched roof to a mobile home

Our trailer started out with a nearly flat roof that allowed water to puddle on top of sagging tin.

Although we haven't put much time or money into rehabbing the interior of our trailer, when we ended up with a little extra cash, Mark and I jumped at the opportunity to improve our roof. Please keep in mind that we're far from professionals, so you'll probably want to seek out a more comprehensive book or expert before you follow our roofing lead. That caveat aside, I thought you might enjoy seeing the choices we made during our recent roofing expedition, since the project highlights some of the unique aspects of trailer repair.

At the same time we added a new roof, we decided to extend the waterproof area in order to replace a ramshackle awning over our door with a real porch.

An earnest DIYer could put a new roof on his or her own trailer, but we opted to hire the same expert who provided the tips for our "Trailer overhauls" section. Bradley has roofed about thirty trailers over the last decade, so we felt confident his techniques would stand the test of time.

Our first choice was whether we wanted to make the roof free-standing (supported by wooden posts that go all the way down to the ground) or whether we would place the new roof directly on top of the trailer. Experts disagree about whether a trailer can handle the weight of a solid roof on its two-by-two studs, with most folks in very snowy climates opting for the use of piers, while people farther south often build the roof directly onto the trailer. Bradley has kept an eye on the trailers he roofed without piers and feels they work fine in our climate, so we decided to follow his lead and keep it simple.

That said, we did complicate the endeavor by including a new porch as part of the roofing project. Covered porches can be a bit tricky to add onto trailers if your land is on a slope since the trailer is close to the ground and has a low ceiling. If you're not careful, by the time your porch roof reaches the uphill end, tall folks like my husband will be bumping their heads. By making the new porch roof part of the trailer roof, we were able to decrease the slope of that section and keep the uphill end above head height.

As with any other kind of roof, you'll need to choose between shingles and metal, which will determine the permissible slope (pitch) of

On larger mobile homes, Bradley usually builds trusses, but our ten-foot-wide trailer was narrow enough to create a pitch by running a two-by-twelve down the center of the trailer and simply setting rafters on top.

the roof. Metal roofing can be much more shallowly pitched—1:12, meaning that the roof rises 1 inch for every 12 inches of horizontal distance, compared to a minimum pitch of 4:12 for shingles. Since we wanted a shallow pitch, we chose a metal roof, which also gave us the bonus of longevity.

Like pitch and material, the choice of color isn't entirely an aesthetic issue. So-called "cool roofs" (often lighter in color) reflect the energy of the sun during hot summer days, lowering cooling bills by up to 15 percent. On the other hand, people who live in cold climates may prefer a dark-colored roof that will soak up the sun's energy and help lower heating bills in the winter. Although we live on the dividing line between areas where hot and cool roofs make sense, I choose not to air-condition our trailer while we *do* add supplemental winter heat, so passive cooling seemed more helpful for reducing the summer "tin-can" effect.

Next, we had to choose between building trusses or making a simpler pitched roof based on a center beam. Bradley usually builds trusses for wider trailers, but he felt that our ten-foot-wide trailer could support simple two-by-four rafters on a two-by-twelve beam running down the middle of the trailer. The center-beam method isn't quite as strong and does focus more weight on the middle of the trailer (which is less structurally sound), so it's not recommended on wider buildings.

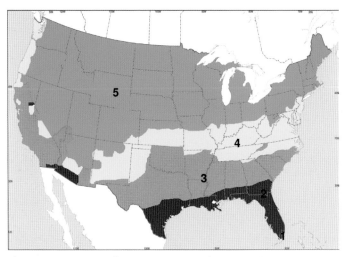

The U.S. Department of Energy recommends R30 to R60 attic insulation and R13 to R30 floor insulation depending on your location.

Zone	Attic Insulation	Floor Insulation
1	R30 to R49	R13
2	R30 to R60	R13 to R19
3	R30 to R60	R19 to R25
4	R30 to R60	R25 to R30
5	R49 to R60	R25 to R30

Another factor that went into planning our roof was my wish for additional insulation. Although we were primarily adding a roof because our current covering kept springing leaks, I hoped to make the project do double-duty by increasing the thermal efficiency of our trailer. The US Department of Energy recommends at least R30 insulation under roofs in our area, with the second table showing the required cavity depth (open space) for various types of insulation.

Minimum cavity depth for fiberglass insulation

R-value	Minimum cavity depth (inches)
R13	3.5
R19	6
R30	9
R38	12

Propping the lower end of the rafters up on a two-by-four gave us room to include R30 insulation underneath most of the roof area.

Bradley planned to keep the weight of our new roof down by framing it with two by fours, but I wanted at least nine inches of space between the old and new roofs so I could insert R30 insulation. In the end, we compromised on eight inches at the lowest end (3.5 inches for each two-by-four plus 1 inch for a furring strip). Compressing the insulation at the very edge of the roof will make it less effective, but since the roof rises as it moves toward the center of the trailer, only the outer rim will be affected. Rather than attaching the insulation to the undersides of the rafters, we treated the space between our two roofs as an attic and laid the insulation flat on the surface of the old roof.

On a shingled roof, you'd need a sheet of plywood on top of the rafters, but for a metal roof, you can simply run a few thin pieces of wood (furring strips) where the tin will be screwed down. (Bradley later cut back the wood close to the chimney to provide adequate clearance.)

Aside from these considerations, framing up our roof was similar to framing any other roof. Bradley first built the box that the rafters would

It's handy to have a station on the ground where you can cut all of the lumber to size before moving it up to the roof.

Although it's possible to put on a roof by yourself, it's easier to have both a ground man and a roof man. (Dogs are optional.)

sit on top of, then screwed the rafters in place, topping them off with furring strips onto which the roofing metal would attach.

The metal itself had to be ordered from the factory a week in advance. We considered using the unglazed roofing panels available at Lowe's and other hardware stores in eight- and ten-foot lengths, but that option would have required a lot more cutting and would have cost more than purchasing roofing directly from the factory. On the other hand, despite longevity claims by the manufacturers, I'm not confident that the glazed coating on housing tin makes up for its thinner metal—only time will tell which type of roofing panel lasts longer.

Drilling a pilot hole on the ground makes tin much easier to attach, but be sure to measure the location of each furring strip so your screws will have something to bite into.

Roofing metal can be ordered in sheets of any size, but you'll sometimes need to cut a sheet or two in half to finish the ends of the roof.

Once the roof is framed up and the metal is prepared, it doesn't take long to screw the panels in place. Be sure to use special roofing screws with gaskets to prevent leaks.

Bradley did 90 percent of the work, but my husband helped out to make the project go more smoothly. Overall, materials cost roughly $1,970 in the summer of 2012 for the 500-square-foot roof plus 200-square-foot porch (decking not included), and we paid Bradley an additional $850 for his labor. At $4 per square foot (in our example), roofing definitely isn't a cheap project, but it's hard to put a price tag on not having to wake up on stormy nights to empty buckets of water that are catching leaks in the hall. I'm also confident that the extra insulation will keep us warmer in the winter and cooler in the summer, making this project a good step in the direction of thermal efficiency.

Simple convertible screen door

Aside from a small addition to house our wood stove (shown in the next chapter), the only other major renovation we've made to our trailer is a screen door. As several other trailer-dwellers mentioned, mobile homes tend to require specialty parts since the doors and windows often aren't the same size as those in traditional houses. In addition, some small trailers (like ours) have doors that open out instead of in, which makes it tough to simply add a screen door onto the outside. Bradley solved this problem by replacing our back door with a convertible screen door—breezy in the summer and warm in the winter.

Two-by-twos, a bit of particle board, a few brackets and screws, and some screen formed the majority of the door.

Styrofoam forms an insulative core within the solid part of the door.

After removing the old door, Bradley measured the frame and built a rectangle out of two-by-twos, being careful to leave a bit of extra room around the new door so it would swing freely. He made the bottom solid (with a cat door), while the top was coated with window screening.

One sheet of Styrofoam insulation was enough to insulate the bottom part of the door and also to create a removable piece that we can stuff behind the screen to close the top part of the door up in cold weather. A piece of particleboard screwed across the screen on the outside finished the winter door so it leaks no more heat than our old arrangement did.

Although you can buy the parts separately, we had a screen-door spring set on hand from a yard sale, so we used the kit to complete our project. A latch, spring, and hinges allowed us to hang the door and close it tightly. Although a door like this isn't lockable, it otherwise fulfills all of the functions of both a screen door and a solid door at a fraction of the cost.

Case study: Remodeling their way into debt-free home ownership

Photo credit: Brian and Stephanie Larsen

"We're a young family striving to live a debt-free, self-sufficient lifestyle," Stephanie explained.

Brian and Stephanie Larsen and their two young children recently moved into a 975-square-foot double-wide in north-central Florida. "The decision to live in a trailer was determined by cost," Stephanie explained. The couple had just spent four years paying off a $60,000 debt, a process that Stephanie described as "a slow and painful time." She said, "Combine that with a bad home-financing experience and we knew we were never going to borrow money again—not for a car, to start a business, or even for a house."

Instead, the couple began saving for a home that they could purchase without going into debt. "We had a short time to save and that's when mobile homes came into the picture," Stephanie continued. "Obviously cheaper than conventional homes, we searched for old trailers that we could renovate. We finally found one, and considering we didn't pay anything for the trailer itself (we made an offer for the land and a few other amenities), we think we got an amazing deal."

Photo credit: Brian and Stephanie Larsen

The double-wide trailer, land, and associated facilities cost $14,500 in 2014.

The couple spent $14,500 on 0.28 acres of land in early 2014, a price that included the 1972-model trailer, a well, septic system, electricity, concrete driveway, carport, and screened-in patio. Since the couple paid cash, they were able to move into their new home with no debt. "Because of our trailer, we are financially free and have an asset," Stephanie declared proudly.

When asked how her friends and family reacted to their decision to move into an old mobile home, she elaborated: "Our friends and family know how we feel about debt and living the 'status quo.' We are not your average family and are not afraid of what other people think about living in trailers. We think people are intrigued about our decision to practice delayed gratification and live mortgage-free in a trailer."

The bathroom was the first item on the couple's renovation agenda. The photo above shows the sink area before renovation . . .

Photo credit: Brian and Stephanie Larsen

. . . and this photo shows the same area after Stephanie and Brian's hard work.

Photo credit: Brian and Stephanie Larsen

Although the couple was pleased to have found a place to live with no mortgage or rent payment, Stephanie was realistic about their new home. "When we first looked at our trailer I didn't like it," she said. "It was small, dated, and dirty. There were boxes, furniture, and clutter still left from the previous owners. The kitchen and bathroom were decrepit, but we did see hope. It was old and dirty, but in excellent, sturdy condition for its age."

As soon as they moved in, the Larsens got to work. First, they remodeled the bathroom, an extensive project that involved installing a new bathtub, toilet, flooring, and sink. Stephanie was quick to explain that the bathroom still needs a new window, trim, and decor, but so far the renovation has only cost the family $750 since they did all of the work themselves. An additional $3,800 invested in a new refrigerator and air conditioner have also helped to improve their standard of living.

The living room is the next item on the couple's renovation agenda.

Photo credit: Brian and Stephanie Larsen

"Currently, we're painting the living room and dining room, adding trim, and new windows and blinds," Stephanie explained.

"We were willing to live in something less desirable in order not to have a payment," Stephanie recalled. "Our trailer is still a work in progress, but I like it better after living here for a little under a year. Even though not even half of the home is remodeled yet, it's cozy and comfortable. We are making it ours."

Improving their mobile home gives the couple an opportunity to "practice our DIY skills," and I could tell that Stephanie was enjoying turning the old space into something fresh and new for her family. On the other hand, she was less excited by the property's small lot size. "We can never have a goat or a cow, and we have neighbors in close proximity to us on every side," Stephanie said.

Her other major complaint with the young trailerstead is the tendency of mobile homes to depreciate in value over time. Since the Larsens consider their trailerstead to be a starter home and eventually plan to sell their current property and "buy something with more land with cash," Stephanie is unsure whether they'll make their money back on their current investment. Similarly, when asked what guidance they'd give to new trailersteaders, the Larsens said: "Our advice would be to not pay more than $10,000 for a mobile home itself no matter how new and big it may be, and that is because mobile homes are a depreciating asset."

Despite the potential for declining property values, though, the Larsens' trailer is currently an excellent place to save, grow, and learn. "The biggest door it opened for us was to be able to live debt- and mortgage-free," Stephanie said. "This is a paid-for starter property."

Read more about the Larsens' adventures as they continue to renovate their mobile home and expand their homestead at www.thewannabehomesteader.com.

HEATING AND COOLING A MOBILE HOME

Is energy use a trailer's Achilles' heel?

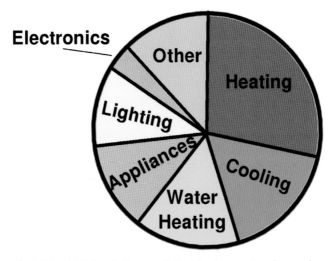

The ENERGY STAR website reports that heating and cooling make up nearly half of the energy bill for the average American home.

While the simplicity of a trailer's construction makes remodeling a breeze, I couldn't help wondering whether trailersteaders were spending far more than they should on energy bills. To answer that question, I turned to the US ENERGY STAR website and discovered that the average American family spends $2,200 per year on energy. In contrast, nearly all of the trailer-dwellers interviewed for this book came in below that average, with annual energy bills ranging from $415 to $2,300, clear proof that usage choices can make a huge difference in your energy consumption regardless of your ability to pay for insulation and energy-star appliances.

But trailer-dwellers have to be especially vigilant in order to lower their energy bills because the deck is stacked against them. Heating and cooling make up almost half of an American's average energy usage, and this is the spot where trailers tend to fare the worst. Thinly insulated walls and roofs let in the summer heat and winter cold quickly, and many trailer-dwellers are afraid to install more sustainable heating options like wood stoves for fear of burning down their mobile home.

I've sprinkled energy-saving tips throughout this book, so if you're flipping around rather than reading straight through, you might want to start your education by reading the relevant sections elsewhere. The case study "Building a house for your trailer" presents one solution for insulating a mobile home, while much of the "Remodeling a trailer" chapter pertains to more mainstream methods of improving a mobile home's insulative and heat-retention properties. This chapter takes up where those sections left off, with passive-solar and energy-efficient heating and cooling choices that work just as well (or better) in trailers as they do in houses.

Low- and no-cost heating and cooling options

Photo credit: Wendy Jehanara Tremayne and Mikey Sklar

Mikey and Wendy use lifestyle changes to keep their trailer cool in the summer.

Since 18 to 20 percent of all heat lost from an average American home comes out the windows and doors (with a similar amount of heat shining in during hot summer months), simple window management can make a big difference in the trailersteader's energy bills. Mikey (profiled in the "Cheap and green" case study) explained how he and his partner use window coverings to lower their summer-cooling costs:

> *"Each day by 2 p.m., we shut out almost all the light from the south and west using two to three layers of curtains. This creates a dark environment that we can cool with a minuscule 300-watt swamp cooler. There are more tricks, like letting the cool morning air in and closing all the windows by 9 a.m. The real win for us has been to block as much west light as possible. Around 7:30 p.m. (sundown), we remove all the layers of curtains, shut off the swamp, and crack the windows."*

When the outside temperature is cooler than the indoor temperature, that's our cue to open windows in the summer.

In our own trailer, we use similar window-management tricks to escape the summer heat. An indoor-outdoor thermometer adds a hint of science to the endeavor and makes it easy to know exactly when to open windows in the evening. As soon as the outdoor temperatures fall below that of our trailer interior, the time has come to open every window (except for west-facing apertures that bear the brunt of the heat from the setting sun). Turning on a window fan at the same time accelerates the movement of cool air into our trailer, and by the time we go to bed (around 10 p.m.), it's nearly always cool enough to sleep beneath a light blanket.

By morning, the open-windowed trailer has cooled down considerably, and that's our cue to close all the windows and pull down the blinds. Even on summer days when outside temperatures are rising into the nineties, the simple act of closing in the nighttime cool is enough to keep indoor temperatures moderate until at least after lunchtime.

David chose to buy quilted window blinds like the one shown above for his main living space. The quilted blinds (sometimes called insulated Roman shades) run on a track and seal all around the window.

You can use a similar technique (but without the window-opening) to maintain interior heat in the winter. Remove coverings from south-facing windows during the day to let the sun's warmth stream in, then use homemade or store-bought window coverings to prevent that heat from radiating back out through the windows at night. The photos here showcase both a store-bought and a homemade option, each of which was installed by David (profiled in the case study "An incognito trailer").

This homemade window covering in the basement of David's house upgrades the R-value of his double-glazed window from R2 to R8 or R9.

Screen doors and window fans are also effective at lowering indoor temperatures in the summer, using much less electricity than air conditioners do. Again, work with nature to make your efforts worthwhile, blocking off screen-door openings during the height of summer days, then opening everything up and turning on the fans once the outside temperatures have cooled down.

Finally, the cheapest way to stay warm in the winter and cool in the summer without breaking the bank is to change your own tolerance levels. Wearing sweaters in the winter and short clothes in the summer gives you a wider range of comfortable room temperatures, and playing chicken with heating and cooling devices during the shoulder seasons will allow your body to adapt to warmer summer temperatures and to colder winter temperatures. You may find yourself content with inside temperatures between 55 and 85 if you wait to turn on the hot and cold air in fall and spring. As an added bonus, some people believe that experiencing a wide range of room temperatures is good for your health and longevity.

Easy DIY window awnings

Homemade awnings allow Harry and Zoe to keep their windows open even during rains.

Photo credit: Harry and Zoe

Harry and Zoe (profiled in the case study "Early retirement in a trailer") live in a 28-by-56-foot mobile home in Virginia. They built awnings onto their residence, using metal roofing material to cover each of their windows. Harry wrote, "The awnings let us keep our windows open during most of the spring and fall, even during heavy rains."

The awnings were constructed using metal roofing, aluminum angle, and treated wood.

Photo credit: Harry and Zoe

"The awning frames are 1-1/2-by-1/8-inch aluminum angle," Harry explained. "The frame sections are held together with 1/4-20 stainless cap screws, with flat washers on both sides of the frame sections, and nylon locking nuts. The awning frames are attached to the wall studs with 1/4-by-4-inch zinc-plated lag screws, with 1-by-2-inch pressure-treated wood-backing strips between the awning frames and the aluminum siding."

Harry mentioned that fresh pressure-treated wood is not recommended for contact with aluminum or galvanized roofing because of the possibility of a chemical reaction. He avoids this potential problem by storing pressure-treated lumber for a year or two before use. "I've been using stale, dry, pressure-treated wood in direct contact with aluminum and galvanized metal for many years, and have never experienced any corrosion problems," Harry added.

As an experienced builder, Harry was able to build and install eight awnings in twelve hours, and he puts in a bit of extra time twice a year to take down the awnings on the east and west walls of his mobile home to prevent damage from ice sliding off the roof. To simplify the annual task (which requires about twenty minutes per awning), Harry leaves in place the lag screws that attach the short piece of aluminum frame to the trailer wall, simply unscrewing the bolts that attach the long frame pieces to the short section of frame.

Window awnings are a great addition to any trailer, shading out the sun and keeping water from damaging the frames of your windows. The overhangs break up the blocky appearance of a mobile home's exterior, and, as Harry mentioned, it's always a plus to be able to keep your windows open during summer thunderstorms so you can enjoy the show of raging water. Finally, the price tag is right—while Harry estimates each of his awnings cost $50 to build with new materials, small pieces of used roofing metal are often available that would lower the price tag even further. This DIY project is definitely within reach for an inexperienced builder who wants to put just a little bit of time and money into making his trailer a better place to live.

Passive-solar heating

Although not a trailer, this house is a perfect example of passive-solar design. Most of the south side of the house consists of a bank of windows, and a grape arbor helps block summer sun.

If you think I'm a bit nutty for suggesting adapting to such a wide range of temperatures, but you don't want to use too much energy to heat and cool your trailer, passive-solar tricks might be right up your alley. Put simply, passive-solar heating refers to collecting the sun's warmth without using solar panels or other electrified devices.

You typically have to think further ahead to take advantage of the sun's energy passively, and you may need to spend a bit more money up front, but the long-term rewards are striking. On sunny winter days, I let our wood stove go out between 11 a.m. and 4 p.m. because the sun's energy is more than enough to keep our inside space warm . . . and I only planned our trailer to take advantage of about a third of the passive-solar gain it could have netted. If you've got a bit more money to put into a passive-solar system, the sun could provide most of your winter heat.

Despite their lack of insulation, single-wide trailers have one thing going for them in the heat department—they are perfectly shaped to take advantage of the energy of the sun. Often, a passive-solar building is designed to be long and skinny, with a panel of windows lining the extensive south side and with few or no windows on the north side. A carefully calibrated roof overhang ensures that the summer sun doesn't find its way through the south-facing windows, but the lower winter sun is still able to shine inside.

(As a quick side note, I should mention that when I talk about "south" and "north" throughout this book in relation to the sun, I'm assuming you reside in the northern hemisphere. Folks down under will instead want to orient their windows toward the north to take advantage of passive-solar gain.)

We used two-by-fours to frame up our new windows rather than sticking with the two-by-twos that originally framed the wall. The wider lumber allowed us to include more insulation.

Adding windows to the south side of a mobile home is remarkably easy. If your trailer is like ours, just unscrew the metal siding on the outside and remove the wooden interior face covering the same area on the inside of the structure. Locate any electrical wiring and carefully move it out of the way (turning off the relevant breaker at the same time), then pull out the insulation and remove the wooden studs. You can use the same wood to frame back up around your new windows and the same inner and outer skins to seal the wall closed, although I recommend fresh insulation inside the renovated wall. The only other factor to consider is sturdiness of the new wall—narrow windows allow you to replace all of the studs that originally supported the roof, or you can use more complicated framing techniques to keep the wall structurally sound when installing wider windows.

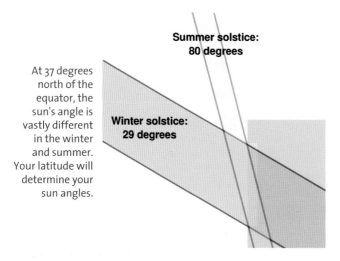

At 37 degrees north of the equator, the sun's angle is vastly different in the winter and summer. Your latitude will determine your sun angles.

Summer solstice: 80 degrees

Winter solstice: 29 degrees

The next step is to make sure you block the summer sun so you don't bake during the warmer months. In the long term, a deciduous shade tree planted in front of the south face of your trailer is the optimal choice since the tree will be leafless during the winter, then, during the summer, it will block sun from entering the windows while also shading your roof. In the short term, though, you'll want to either erect a trellis lined with fast-growing plants, to build shutters or wooden blinds for the outside of your trailer, or to install a roof overhang just the right width to let in the winter sun but to shut out energy from the higher summer sun.

When planning a permanent awning or roof overhang, first decide during which part of the year you want to have sun striking your windows. Many passive-solar engineers use the time between the fall and spring equinoxes as a basic rule of thumb, but you'll want to shorten that time if you live in a very warm area and lengthen it if you live in a very cold climate. Next, use the calculator at susdesign.com/sunangle/ to determine the angle of your sun at the cutoff date—at our latitude, the sun angle is 52.75 degrees at noon on March 21. Now measure the vertical distance between the bottom of the roof overhang and the bottom of the window (five feet in our case) and use some basic geometry to determine the length of your overhang.

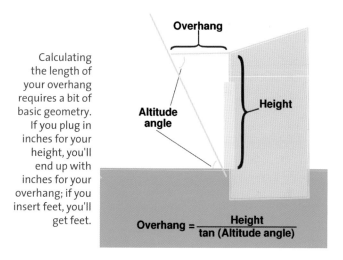

Calculating the length of your overhang requires a bit of basic geometry. If you plug in inches for your height, you'll end up with inches for your overhang; if you insert feet, you'll get feet.

$$\text{Overhang} = \frac{\text{Height}}{\tan (\text{Altitude angle})}$$

In the case of my example, my overhang should be 46 inches long if I want to totally shade my window between the two equinoxes. A smaller overhang will give me shade during a shorter portion of the year, while a wider overhang will give me shade for longer.

The final feature of a well-designed passive-solar system is some sort of thermal mass inside the trailer to capture the energy from the winter sun and radiate that warmth back out into the room at night. We haven't installed anything yet, but plan to eventually tile the floor in front of our bank of windows as a heat battery. Other materials with a high thermal mass include concrete, brick, clay, and containers of water, all of which will help mitigate hot summer days as well as cold winter nights.

Despite the slightly scary math, the actual renovations necessary to convert a trailer over to take advantage of passive-solar heating can be well within the reach of the beginning DIYer as long as you plan the trailer's orientation properly during installation. As an added bonus, you'll notice that the windows light the interior of your trailer with no need for electric lamps between dawn and dusk—yet more energy savings!

Shade trellis to cool your home with plants

Scarlet runner beans provided fast summer shade while also attracting hummingbirds to the flowers and feeding us with their fruits.

I was so taken by Rebecca's trellis (shown in the case study "Hiding in the vegetation") that I decided Mark and I needed one of our own. Our bank of south-facing windows does a great job of heating our living space during the winter, but the sun continues to shine in during parts of the shoulder season when we'd prefer to promote cool air instead. While we could build a solid awning to block that sun, using plants for shade has the benefit of more closely matching the seasons—when the leaves are present on tender perennials like grapes, we want shade, and when the leaves are absent, we want sun.

Our south-facing bank of windows allowed sun to shine in during parts of the year that weren't optimal for its passive-solar purpose.

Rather than waiting for a rain, it's handy to test gutters using a bucket of water. If the liquid doesn't quickly flow to the downspout, then the downspout end of the gutter needs to be lowered.

Our first attempt at blocking out the summer sunlight with plants was a dismal failure because I didn't take into account the waterlogged nature of soil close to a gutterless trailer. Luckily, my first year's experiment involved annual beans and peas, so it was no huge loss when every plant I seeded failed to grow. But the experience did prompt me to take steps to dry up that space before moving forward with my trellis project.

How can you tell if you need to follow my lead at terraforming before trellising? If you're not sure whether the ground beside your trailer is too wet to plant into, dig a hole in the trellis location the day after a heavy rain. If liquid is located within an inch or two of the surface after the storm ends, then you need to deal with excess water before you can invest in any plants.

Elevating the soil is a tried-and-true method of drying up wet ground. We widened a path elsewhere and used the soil we excavated to build the raised bed in front of our trailer.

There are two methods you can use to dry up ground right beside your trailer, and I recommend using both in tandem if you live in a particularly wet climate like ours. First, you can add gutters to your roof, then channel the excess moisture downhill and away from your mobile home. Hanging gutters is neither complicated nor expensive, but the use of a level will be a major boon if your trailer, like ours, has a slight slope that makes gutter tilt counterintuitive. After getting the angle of our gutter right (third try's the charm!), we used corrugated piping to transfer the rain water from the roof to our greywater wetland. (See the section "Greywater wetland" for more details.)

Another method of drying up wet garden soil is to elevate the earth using raised beds. In our vegetable garden, I usually build wall-less mounds in wet areas, but since the area in front of our trailer is our primary outdoor living room, I decided to splurge and use an old railroad tie (purchased used for $5) to edge the bed in this location.

As a side note, railroad ties and other treated wood will last a long time in the moist environment of the soil, but both can add nasty chemicals to your ground. Of the two options, recycled railroad ties are probably the safer choice since most of the leachable chemicals have already fled from the wood during the many years that the ties spent exposed to weather on the railroad track. Plus, creosote doesn't contain heavy metals, which are the one kind of contaminant that healthy soil microorganisms can't break down into harmless by-products. Of course, if you don't mind replacing your edging at intervals, untreated wood will be an even safer choice and will add humus to your soil as it rots away.

The first step in building our trellis consisted of screwing eye bolts into a piece of lumber.

Mark attached the board to our wood-stove alcove to support one side of the trellis.

A turnbuckle made it easy to add tension to the wire.

We still had too much give to the wire though, so we added a two-by-four spacer.

The completed trellis casts very little shade during the winter months, but the structure will be able to support two mature grapevines to provide summer shade.

With the water situation taken care of, I asked my husband to build an overhead trellis to support the eventual vines I planned to grow. We originally considered building the trellis out of wood, but in the end we chose wire instead since the thin strands are less likely to block winter sun. The 10-gauge wire we used is the same thickness often found in grape trellises, so we felt comfortable asking the metal strands to hold up quite a few plants. Other materials that went into the trellis included large eye bolts, turnbuckles, one carabiner (because our second eye bolt ended in a loop instead of a hook), and treated 2-by-6-inch lumber.

Our shade trellis happens to be in a handy location for arbor-building since the area has walls on three sides—the wood-stove addition on the west, a porch on the east, and the trailer on the north. Mark was able to attach a piece of pressure-treated lumber to the wood-stove addition and to the porch, then he drilled holes in one of the pieces of lumber and used eye bolts in the other piece to convert lengths of wire into four plant-support strands. Tension was achieved using turnbuckles that shorten as they twist, and a carabiner made one turnbuckle easy to attach to its eye bolt.

Although we did manage to achieve good tension in our trellis eventually, we probably would build the structure slightly differently if we repeated the project. In the end, we were forced to slip a couple of scrap pieces of two-by-fours under the looped part of the wire to add yet more tension to the overhead trellis wire, which wasn't the optimal solution. Part of our tensioning problem was caused by using recycled wire full of kinks, so quite a bit of the turnbuckles' shortening power was wasted straightening the wire. If we built another arbor, we would definitely splurge and start with fresh wire. Another way to simplify the tensioning part of the project would be to make each trellis line out of a separate piece of wire rather than wrapping one piece of wire around to make two trellis lines—the looped wire was tougher to tension than it needed to be. All of that said, though, it was relatively simple to achieve tension even using our technique, and the whole project only took a few hours.

Young vines can be trained to grow toward an overhead trellis using a piece of twine.

As I finish writing this book, perennial plants are just beginning to colonize our shade trellis. I chose a grape for one corner and a hardy kiwi for the other side, and have been thrilled by the way the grapevine quickly twined up a piece of string to reach the overhead trellis over the course of one summer. The hardy kiwi was a less-appropriate selection since the species didn't appear to enjoy the high-heat environment promoted by summer sun reflecting off the metal walls of the trailer, so we may end up replacing it with another grape. Other perennial vines that I haven't tested in this situation but that have edible possibilities include hops (hardy to zone 3), rugosa roses (hardy to zone 3), akebia (hardy to zone 4, but reported to be invasive in Kentucky, Maryland, New Jersey, Pennsylvania, Virginia, and the District of Columbia, so plant with caution), and passionflowers (some varieties are hardy to zone 5, but even the hardiest varieties will die back to the ground every year in zones 5 and 6). Of course, if your heart isn't set on edibles, many ornamental vines exist as well, including wisteria, clematis, non-rugosa climbing roses, and trumpet vine.

The first year, perennial vines don't tend to grow much, so I recommend filling in the extra space with annuals. A month after planting, our scarlet runner beans were already starting to coat their trellises.

Although established perennial vines have the advantage of quickly leafing out to cover a shade trellis in the spring, the old adage "first they sleep, next they creep, and then they leap" is very true. In other words, you probably shouldn't expect perennial vines to provide appreciable shade until the third year after planting. In the interim, you can fill up that space with fast-growing annual vegetable vines, like runner beans, melons, and gourds. We planted scarlet runner beans during our trellis's first year for a combination of beauty and functionality, and we also added a couple of tomatoes in between, taking advantage of the overhead wires to string-train the tomatoes and create an elegant and delicious growing area.

While many trailersteaders will probably landscape around their trailer immediately, I tend to value utility over aesthetics, thus the lack of skirting and planting around most of our trailer as I type these words. However, even utilitarian-minded trailersteaders like me would do well to consider basic landscaping sooner rather than later. Once I began planting around the base of our trailer, I was immediately thrilled by how much more homey the area felt, and as an added bonus, I now get to botanize out my window. In fact, if you have a species you want to learn more about, I highly recommend a window-side planting location for easy observation of the plant's ecology.

Scarlet runner beans and permaculture tacos

Scarlet runner beans are both ornamental and edible.

I've tried growing several supposedly edible annual vines, and my favorite for both utility and flavor has been scarlet runner beans (*Phaseolus coccineus*). The species is technically a perennial (just like tomatoes and peppers), but unless you live in the Deep South, your vines will perish every year and you'll need to start over from seed. Luckily, the huge seeds sprout very quickly and the resulting plants will grow up strings and reach your roof within a couple of months if growing conditions are favorable.

Scarlet runner beans are very attractive to insect pollinators and hummingbirds, but also to Mexican bean beetles.

Why am I so fond of scarlet runner beans? In addition to their vigorous growth, the plants provide edible beans (more on these below) and beautiful red flowers. The latter are magnets for insects and hummingbirds, and I've spent many enjoyable hours watching wildlife consume the beans' nectar and pollen. Unfortunately, scarlet runner beans are also very attractive to the garden pest Mexican bean beetle, so be sure to plant your ornamentals a distance away from the vegetable garden if you prefer not to use insecticides.

We enjoy turning scarlet runner beans into a sort of bean paste, then assembling so-called Permaculture Tacos.

Scarlet runner beans are edible in the green bean, lima bean, and dried bean stages, although you should be sure to cook them to remove the poisonous compounds found in all beans (which are most concentrated in scarlet runner beans and in kidney beans). The starchy roots and tender flowers are also reputed to be edible. My husband is a very tentative dried-bean-eater, but the recipe below for Permaculture Tacos really hit the spot.

Bean paste:

- 1 heaping cup of scarlet runner beans in the lima-bean stage, pods removed
- 1 cup of homemade chicken broth
- 2 small sweet red peppers, minced
- 4 small sprigs of fresh thyme
- 1 large clove of garlic, minced
- salt and pepper
- olive oil (about 1/4 cup, enough to make the consistency hummusy)
- 1 large handful of dried tomatoes, on the soft side rather than thoroughly dried
- 1 small handful of walnuts

Other ingredients:

- Malabar-spinach leaves
- Arugula, chopped
- Tomatoes, thinly sliced
- Sweet red peppers, thinly sliced
- Edible-pod peas, thinly sliced
- (Or whatever salad ingredients you have in your garden. Use your imagination!)

Cook the beans, peppers, thyme, and garlic in the chicken broth for about 20 minutes, until the beans are soft. (Unfortunately, the brilliant color goes away during this stage and the beans turn gray.) Cool, then puree the mixture in the food processor with the other bean-paste ingredients. Serve as little tacos made out of the Malabar-spinach leaves filled with bean paste and vegetables. These can be eaten with one hand like a soft taco if you're careful not to overfill, and they make a festive and delicious vegetable side or appetizer.

Wood heat

Playing with fire

Don't forget to sift the charcoal out of your wood ashes and use the former on the garden. Read more about biochar in *The Weekend Homesteader*.

No matter how careful you are to optimize the passive-solar potential of your trailer, in most parts of the United States, you'll still need to add some type of supplemental heat. After some experimentation, Mark and I settled on an efficient wood stove as a self-sufficient and cheap way to heat our home.

Installing a wood stove in a mobile home may seem like playing with fire, but the truth is that any heating option has the potential to burn your house down. If you choose an energy-efficient wood stove and harvest the firewood sustainably, wood heat can be an economical and environmentally friendly option, and careful installation of the stove will ensure that it is no less safe than a wood stove in a stick-built home.

Exterior furnace

Our first foray into wood heat was an exterior furnace, which was arguably safer than an interior wood stove, but was definitely less efficient.

When we first dipped a tentative toe into the concept of wood heat, Mark and I began our experimentation with an exterior wood furnace. I can't really recommend this option, but I thought I'd throw the idea out there so that others can learn from our mistakes. On the plus side, we did learn a lot about wood heat, and the stove did lower our electric bill enough to pay for itself in the first year. But the disadvantages were many.

The color of the smoke coming out of your chimney is an indicator of a wood stove's efficiency. Darker smoke means a less efficient fire and more air pollution.

As the name suggests, an exterior furnace keeps the fire safely outside your home, then you pipe the heat into the house using water lines or (in our case) air ducts. The trouble is that you also lose a lot of heat to the outdoors, and none of the furnace options I've seen are very energy efficient to begin with, so you end up burning a lot of wood. The $200 furnace we found on eBay was also a bear to start and churned out sooty smoke once the fire was raging. As a final mark against exterior wood furnaces, you have to run a fan or pump to get heat from your furnace into the house, meaning that your wood stove does little good during power-outage situations. After ten days without electricity one snowy winter, we decided to shift gears.

Mobile-home wood-stove requirements

Heating with wood helps the homesteader take another step toward independence.

Even though our exterior furnace was a failure, we still liked the idea of wood heat. So we were thrilled when a bit of research determined that it's quite possible to install a wood stove inside a mobile home. The differences between mobile-home and traditional-home installation come down to six main requirements for the former:

- A close-clearance (double-walled) pipe must be used to connect the stove to the chimney.
- Spark arresters should be installed in the chimney cap.

- The stove should be grounded to the home chassis.

- The stove must have tie-downs to attach it to the floor so it won't shift around when the trailer is moved. (Presumably, this is only relevant if your trailer will actually be moved again.)

- The stove should use exterior air for combustion.

- Wood stoves are not permissible in mobile-home bedrooms.

Small stoves are a good fit in a mobile home. Although expensive, we feel like our Jotul F 602 was worth the price tag—we now use a fraction of the wood that the exterior furnace consumed and keep our trailer warmer in the process.

(As usual, it's best to check your local building codes to make sure there are no local additions or changes to the list above.)

Another factor to consider is choosing a wood stove that's approved for use in a mobile home. In general, these stoves are on the small to medium side, have a top-exiting flue collar (meaning the stove pipe comes out the top of the stove rather than the back), and include a heat shield on the back. These characteristics combine to make the clearance around all sides of the stove less, which in turn lets them fit into the small spaces found in a typical mobile home. In fact, I learned that the small size of mobile homes is really the biggest danger feature, so your goal should be to find a spot for your wood stove where you can provide plenty of open air space around it. The stove model you choose will list the minimum clearance requirements on each side—plan to attain or exceed those standards.

An efficient wood stove saves money and prevents pollution. As you can see, the smoke coming out of our chimney is perfectly clear as long as the wood we burn is dry.

Small stoves simply make sense in a small home anyway since you get the most heat and the least pollution per piece of firewood if you don't damp your stove down and instead let each piece of wood burn fast and hot. Although it's only a rough guide, many sources suggest planning on 50 to 55 BTU of stove output per square foot of living area in the extreme north of the United States, 30 to 35 BTU per square foot in the Deep South, and around 40 to 45 BTU per square foot in the middle of the country. Using those guidelines, our 500-square-foot trailer requires a wood stove rated at 2,000 to 2,250 BTU—your trailer may need a little bit more or less output depending on your own circumstances.

Installing a wood stove

Adding a small alcove to our trailer made it easy to ensure our stove had plenty of clearance.

Since our trailer is so small, we opted to begin our wood-stove adventure by building on a small alcove to house the stove, planning the size around the minimum clearances with use of heat shields. If we ever planned to move our trailer, the alcove would obviously be a bad idea, but it was a cheap and relatively easy option for keeping the wood stove out of the main traffic flow of our house, and for ensuring that only nonflammable materials came close to the fire hazard.

We used old roofing metal spaced an inch away from the wall as homemade heat shields.

If you're cramped for space (and in most mobile homes you will be), heat shields are a helpful way of lowering your safe clearance distances. (Your wood stove will usually list minimum clearances with and without heat shields.) Although you can buy expensive heat shields at the wood-stove store, a heat shield is really just a piece of metal with plenty of room for air to flow behind it. Noncombustible spacers hold the metal an inch away from the wall and hot air flows in behind the metal from down at the floor, past the stove, and out the top. The result is that the wall behind the heat shield never gets hot enough to catch on fire, although the heat shields will feel quite warm to the touch when your stove is roaring.

A ceiling support kit, available for around $300 or less from a store like Lowe's, will expedite wood-stove installation.

Putting a ceiling support kit into a new addition makes installation even easier since you can build around the parts you have rather than trying to make the parts fit between existing rafters.

Although expensive, stainless-steel, double-walled chimney pipe is a good safety feature. As a bonus, the metal won't rot out in a year or two like single-walled stove pipe often does in wet climates.

Be sure to pick up a tube of high-temperature caulk to prevent rain from seeping down your chimney pipe.

After planning the clearances, we needed to consider how we'd attach the chimney to the roof of the alcove. Starting with a ceiling support kit (plus extra pieces of stove pipe for a total cost of $261 in 2010) makes this part of the project feasible for a moderately skilled DIYer. You can cut costs (although with the side effect of lowering safety margins) if you cobble together these pieces yourself; conversely, you'll spend a lot more on the chimney components if you buy them from the wood-stove store.

Your stove paperwork will list minimum clearances in each direction for the nonflammable hearth as well as for proximity to walls. Typically, you need to allow a bit more room in front since sparks can fly out the wood stove's door.

With the ceiling support kit and chimney in place, it's time to move on to the floor protection. A piece of nonflammable cement board topped by inexpensive ceramic tiles will prevent the stove from overheating the materials beneath it, and will ensure that flying sparks don't catch your trailer on fire. Our floor covering cost about $25.

Our energy-efficient wood stove is the best investment we've made in increasing our comfort levels.

We opted to jack our stove up onto solid cinder blocks rather than cutting a piece of stove pipe to just the right length to slide in between the ceiling support kit and the stove collar.

No matter how you install your stove, be sure to lift with your legs not your back—even tiny wood stoves are heavy! If you bought a brand-new stove, my last piece of advice is to try to install it during warm weather so you can light your first few fires with all of the trailer's windows open. Stoves are usually treated with a substance that creates a foul odor when it first reaches high heat. Similarly, be sure to read the stove's instructions carefully—our manufacturer recommended that we start with a few small and medium fires before heating the stove to full roar, and the booklet also gave tips for the best way to light fires in our individual model.

If we could go back in time and make one addition to our trailer earlier than we made it in real life, the wood stove would be on the top of the list (followed by a shady porch on the north side for summer dining). Assuming you live in a cold-winter area, I highly recommend an efficient wood stove for lower energy use and winter basking.

Case study: "A crazy, cobbled-together, split-level mobile home"
A small home for a large family

Photo credit: Lindsey and Keith

A pavilion-style roof protects two joined trailers.

Lindsey and her husband Keith live in a "crazy, cobbled-together, split-level mobile home" in northeast Alabama with their five children. "We also have another baby due in February 2013, and we hope to have several more before my child-bearing days are over," Lindsey added. At 1,680 square feet, personal space in their two-trailer combo clocks in below the average size of even a 1950s-era home, but they find that the advantages of trailer life outweigh the disadvantages.

Lindsey and Keith's family in 2010.

"We moved from western Washington State to Georgia in 2002 with our 7-month-old firstborn, hoping to find a place where we could live on one income and buy some land," said Lindsey. "Being willing to live in a trailer certainly enables us to live the way we do, on one income with Mom homeschooling the kids. That was our priority and we were willing to do just about anything to achieve that."

Cobbling together a trailer combo

The two trailers are joined by a connecting stairway, cut on Christmas Eve 2011. "It was a great gift!" Lindsey recalled.

"When we found a real-estate ad for eleven acres with a 'house' for $40,000 we immediately made an appointment to see it," Lindsey remembered. The house turned out to be a 10-by-40-foot trailer from the early 1960s with a "poorly-built addition of about the same size," which they later tore down.

"Our plan was to live in the trailer/addition combo for 5 to 10 years while saving money to build a more suitable house," Lindsey said. "There was always a sort of 'ew, a trailer' attitude between us, although we didn't look down on other folks who lived in them. We just figured we'd need something sturdier and bigger for the family we were hoping to grow."

But the trailer slowly won the family over. "The little trailer had a really good design that took advantage of every bit of available space in a relatively attractive way," Lindsey explained. "Well, we liked it anyway. And my husband always admired how well-designed things were for such a small space."

Photo credit: Lindsey and Keith

You can see both trailers in this photo, taken during the construction of the roof. "The smaller trailer is almost centered on the larger one lengthwise, so there's about the same amount of offset at the other end," Lindsey explained.

Perhaps because of the positive aspects of the original trailer, the couple opted to increase their living area by adding a second trailer, purchased for $7,500 and moved and installed for another $3,000. "Our second trailer is a 1998 model 16x80. It's not as well planned as the older trailer. I think it tries too hard not to look like a trailer."

The roof allowed room for an extensive covered porch, which is still under construction.

With the two trailers butting up against each other, the obvious next step was to turn them into a single structure with a joined roof. "The roof is pretty colossal and ended up costing a lot more time, money, and effort than we initially imagined," Lindsey said, adding that the final price tag for the roof alone was close to $9,500. "So we probably could have purchased a place with a more typical home for the money we've spent, but we wouldn't have the space we have now, we wouldn't have a unique home (which we like!), and we would still be in debt instead of having spent the money when we had it, a little (and sometimes a lot) at a time."

Kids in a trailer

Lindsey's daughter, then four years old, standing in a hole dug for one of the roof supports.

"We homeschool our children, so six of us are home pretty much all day long, five or six days per week. That means that our house takes more abuse than most folks', just because everything gets used so much more often. We've replaced our stove twice and repaired our fridge at least three times. The toilet gets flushed and the doors get opened (but seldom closed) much more often."

When asked about the disadvantages of trailer life, Lindsey pointed to the tendency of their home to break at inopportune moments, along with the lack of resale value. But she added the caveat: "We don't have plans to leave our place, so that isn't really an issue for us."

The four oldest children sleep in bunk beds built into what used to be the closets.

Photo credit: Lindsey and Keith

Lack of space was more of a problem before adding the larger trailer, so the pair buried a 10-by-40-foot shipping container in the yard for storage. "The shipping container helped me keep my sanity," Lindsey recalled. "Now it serves as a tornado shelter as well as a food-storage space and a place to keep out-of-season or outgrown clothes and child-related equipment." Lindsey plans to use the shipping container as a root cellar as well, since being sunk in the ground "gives it a little extra cool factor."

Unconventional heating and cooling

"This is the connecting opening from the top side (larger trailer)," Lindsey said. "Just beyond the red lampshade in the background is where we have the wood stove. We keep a fan hanging from the ceiling in this opening (the space is at least 4 feet wide) to keep warm air circulating."

In northern Alabama, winters can be chilly and summers are scorching, so both heating and cooling are an issue. The family averages about $150 per month on electricity, which includes running two window air conditioners for six to eight weeks in the summer. An additional $150 per year provides propane for cooking, and "hubby and the boys cut, haul, split, and stack our firewood, so there's no real cost there except oil, gas, and new chains," Lindsey said. "Our energy costs are still quite manageable, and since we don't have a mortgage any longer, it's definitely cost-effective for us to live in a less energy-efficient home."

"We do a lot of drying laundry outdoors, but we go through seasons (especially with a new baby and only little kids to 'help') of using our dryer more than we'd like, and we pay for that," Lindsey said about her electricity use. "Now that I have two who are more capable of helping in that area, we don't use [the dryer] nearly as much."

Although Lindsey's trailers are not as well-insulated as their neighbors' stick-built houses, the unique roof (and nearby trees) do a great job deflecting summer heat. "Our pavilion-style roof makes it a lot cooler in our house than it would be with a conventional roof," Lindsey said. "We have friends with a trailer almost identical to our newer one. They have zero trees and the original roof and they spend a fortune on cooling it all summer long—for 4 or 5 months—because it just doesn't keep its cool like ours does."

Closing thoughts

Lindsey working on a temporary porch outside the front door.

Photo credit: Lindsey and Keith

I was fascinated by the way Lindsey's attitude toward her trailer changed over the years. "It's been a while in coming, but I think we all like our home," she said. "It's different, more than a little counter-cultural, so to speak, and that's how we like to roll.

"Most people hear about our house and look like they want to move a few feet further away from me, but once they see it or hear more about it they tend to think it's actually kind of cool, if not something they'd ever choose for themselves." She concluded: "A few years before we finished paying off our land, we realized that we're actually not 'too good' to live in a trailer, possibly forever."

AROUND THE TRAILERSTEAD

How is a trailerstead different from a homestead?

Our domicile has grown over the years and now includes a stick-built addition and three porches.

My self-published edition of *Trailersteading* stopped at the boundaries of our trailer, leaving the surrounding homestead as fodder for other books. When the time came to revise the story for print publication, though, I wanted to include a bit of information that wasn't strictly relevant to the physical structure of the mobile home. On the other hand, once I got started writing about rain barrels and composting toilets, what was to prevent me from telling you about our vegetable garden, our chickens, and our honeybees? Why not write about our new dairy goats, our high-density-apple experiments, and our mushroom logs?

And while it might have been safer not to branch out beyond the trailer in the first place, failing to tell you about the greywater wetland that we piped directly into our kitchen sink would make me feel like I was offering up a story that cuts off at the climax with no epilogue. So I decided to leave this chapter in the finished book, but I'm going to do my very best to stick to the point, focusing only on projects directly relating to our mobile-home existence. After you finish reading this chapter, assuming you're still interested in learning about our less trailer-related endeavors, you can head over to our blog at www.WaldenEffect.org for daily updates on our homesteading adventures that reach out further beyond the trailer.

So, what makes a trailerstead different from a homestead built around a house? I've written about most of the differences between these two scenarios previously, but it's worth quickly rehashing the most relevant points here to give you an idea of what I'm talking about. If you're willing to build your homestead around a trailer, chances are you value utility over aesthetics, and you probably don't have nearby neighbors (or pesky building inspectors) who are going to roll their eyes at your crazy experiments. In addition, your initial residence was probably pretty bare-bones, lacking typical features like gutters and porches, and your home's internal square footage is likely to be on the small side. So how can you work with those benefits and liabilities to make your trailerstead even more sustainable than a homestead based around a house? Keep reading for a few examples that should get your own creative juices flowing.

Rain barrels

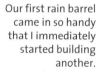
Our first rain barrel came in so handy that I immediately started building another.

I avoided installing rain barrels for years, and now I wish that I hadn't waited so long. Part of my excuse was quite valid—lack of guttering on our trailer made the project much harder than it would be for the average house-dweller. However, I also believed that I wouldn't get much utility from the collected rainwater. After all, our region enjoys about an inch of precipitation per week, so what good would an extra 55 gallons do?

If placed correctly, the answer is "A lot!" as I learned when a friend invited me to a rain-barrel workshop held by a local municipality. I brought home a free barrel, installed it on the porch near where we'd recently put in gutters . . . and fell in love.

Our new rain barrel is located closer to two of our chicken coops than our main spigots are, so the barrel saves me about half an hour of weekly water lugging during peak chicken season in the summer. Added to that energetic savings, I soon discovered that the barrel also comes in handy for washing filthy hands and bare feet that would otherwise be tracking garden grime into the house. (I'd like to say this latter discovery saved me hours of cleaning, but I don't really clean our trailer on a regular basis. Still, the rain barrel made our living conditions nicer between my infrequent sweepings.)

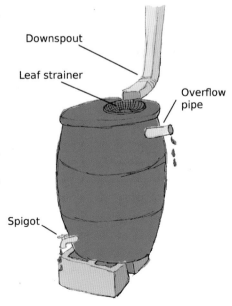

The basic rain barrel consists of a 55-gallon drum elevated on two cinder blocks. Features include a spigot to release water at the bottom of the barrel, a screened entrance to capture water from the gutter downspout, and an overflow pipe near the top.

Downspout

Leaf strainer

Overflow pipe

Spigot

If you don't want your rain barrel to overflow from the top during downpours, your overflow pipe should have the same capacity as your gutter downspout.

Since I've already written about the basics of rain-barrel construction in *The Weekend Homesteader*, I won't repeat that information here. Suffice it to say that a frugal trailersteader can find the parts to build a rain barrel for around $25, or you can buy a rain barrel that's ready-made for about $100. However, I did want to share some tips you won't find elsewhere to make your rain-barrel project a little more efficient.

As you've probably noticed from the photos in this section, I used the very laziest method of installing our rain barrel—I simply set the container on the edge of our front porch. The upside of that technique is that our barrel was automatically elevated high enough to let me place a bucket underneath the spigot, and the water is located in a high-traffic area where it gets put to a lot of use. However, a porch-mounted rain barrel is held to a much higher standard when it comes to leaks than you'd require from a rain barrel simply set on cinder blocks in the yard. That's how I discovered the major flaw in our workshop-built rain barrel's plan—a small overflow pipe.

In the municipality's defense, even store-bought rain barrels tend to share this failing. But as you can see from the photo above, if the overflow pipe on your rain barrel is smaller than the capacity of your

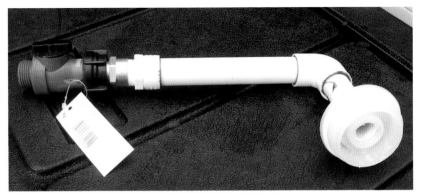

Richard Tidyman is a Career and Technology teacher in North Carolina, and over the years he has developed a cheap and easy rain barrel that's perfect for teaching construction skills to his classes. Richard starts with used barrels that he finds at car washes and dealerships for $10, he turns each barrel upside down, then he uses one of the bung plugs to attach a water-tight, homemade spigot. Parts used to assemble the spigot include PVC-pipe sections and fittings, a brass adapter that changes the 3/4-inch PVC thread to 3/4-inch garden-hose thread, and a full-flow shutoff valve. For full construction details, go to www.youtube.com/watch?v=LseSRUjZJM4.

gutter downspout, your barrel will gush over from the top during heavy rains. I committed to manually moving our inflow pipe away from the barrel every time the barrel overfills as a very low-work solution, but if you're building a rain barrel from scratch, a 4-inch piece of corrugated pipe (like I used to channel water from the downspout to the rain barrel) would be a better selection for an overflow pipe.

Another flaw I discovered in the common rain-barrel plan involves screwing a spigot into the side of the barrel. We learned the hard way that, even after using plumber's tape, the plastic of the barrel is too thin to properly seal around the threads of the spigot in this application. The resulting drip from the point where the faucet connects to the barrel is relatively minor, but if it bothers you, a solution exists. Why not turn the barrel upside-down before modifying it, allowing you to screw a PVC pipe into one of the bung holes for a leak-free spigot? In addition to keeping all of the water in your rain barrel where it belongs, the upside-down rain barrel has the advantage of allowing the user to more thoroughly empty the barrel, which prevents mosquito breeding and speeds the job of draining the reservoir for the winter. The only downside is that you have to get a bit more creative when elevating an upside-down rain barrel, but well-spaced cinder blocks can do the trick as the photo here illustrates.

A rubber connector and PVC pieces make it simple to manage water coming out of an IBC tank.

If you want to collect more than 55 gallons of water, you have two options—daisy chain multiple barrels together or track down a used IBC tank. The average 3-cubic-foot IBC tank holds 275 gallons of water

Photo credit: Brian Cooper, taken at the Little Rock Zoo

Daisy chaining multiple rain barrels together expands your water storage capacity.

and can sometimes be bought used for as little as $25. Just be sure you know what was carried within the tank to discover whether a simple wash with warm water is sufficient to make your high-capacity rain barrel safe to use for watering the garden and livestock. The image on the previous page shows the method our local hardware store attendant suggested for adding a spigot to the base of our IBC tank without taking the trouble to match the threads.

The other option for expanding rain-barrel capacity—daisy chaining—is equally straightforward. You can either create a system where all of the barrels are fed from a central point, or you can use the overflow pipe of the previous barrel to fill each subsequent barrel. The latter option is especially handy if you want to have several reservoirs scattered around your trailerstead, making it easy to decant water at various locations. Just be sure to place each downstream rain barrel lower than the initial rain barrel beneath your gutter so that water will passively flow to fill each reservoir up.

Before I end this section, I'd be remiss if I didn't include a few words on the safety of using water from a rain barrel to hydrate your garden and animals. I wish I could give you a definitive yes or no answer here, but there's currently a lack of consensus on this issue. The best data comes from an extensive study carried out by the Texas Water Development Board involving various roofing materials. In their publication "Effect of Roof Material for Water Quality for Rainwater Harvesting Systems," the authors reported that the first flush entering a rain barrel from any type of roof contains the majority of both the microbial and chemical contaminants. As a result, if you're willing to complicate your rain-barrel-building project, adding a first-flush diverter can eliminate the most problematic rain from your system.

Even with a first-flush diverter, though, later rainwater will still contain more turbidity, total coliform, fecal coliform, iron, and aluminum than is recommended by the EPA for human drinking water. A partial solution to this problem (if you're starting from scratch) is to choose a roofing material with rain barrels in mind. Many experts veto shingles for rainwater collection, even if the water is only being used on your garden. The biggest contaminant concerns with this type of roof seem to be copper, zinc, lead, chromium, arsenic, and polyaromatic hydrocarbons leaching out of the shingles, and the grit that comes off the roofing is also an annoyance in rain-barrel systems. Other roofing materials that some websites recommend avoiding include galvanized metal (which sheds zinc), any kind of roofing treated to prevent moss growth (which sheds copper), and flashing made of copper or lead. In the end, you should use your own judgment before using water from a rain barrel on living things, but I will report that our chickens and ducks seem to thrive on the water that runs off our coated metal roof.

Greywater wetland

A year and a half after its creation, our greywater wetland turns wastewater into a patch of wildlife habitat.

The previous section showed how you can collect free water to use around your homestead, and this section is the flip side of the coin— what to do with dirty water you no longer need. If you don't use the techniques mentioned here, wastewater costs money to dispose of, whether that money comes out of your taxes when you flush effluent from your toilet into the public sewage system, or whether the cash comes straight out of your pocket when you pay to install and service a household septic tank. Meanwhile, that financial cost is coupled with damage to the environment since considerable energy and chemicals are used in mainstream treatment processes. On the other hand, if you separate your greywater from your blackwater, you can treat the former for next to nothing and give the environment a leg up in the process.

Okay, I know I just threw some technical terms at you, so let's back up. Greywater is liquid that you wouldn't want to drink or wash with, but that probably wouldn't make you sick if it splattered across your bare skin. In a typical household, greywater comes from sinks, bathtubs, and washing machines, with the water from the kitchen sink being the dirtiest of these sources. (We've had no trouble using kitchen-sink water in our greywater wetland, but you'd want to be more careful of this source if you were making a more complicated treatment setup than the one I mention below.) In contrast, blackwater comes from your toilet, includes human waste, and needs to be disposed of much more carefully. Although some municipalities do use wetlands a bit like the one I showcase in this chapter to treat blackwater, you probably won't want to do so on the backyard scale because the risk of spreading disease is simply too high.

Photo credit: Barbara Ervin

In a dry climate, greywater can mean the difference between dead grass (left) and healthy grass and asparagus (right).

The frugal homesteader will be glad to learn that separating out your greywater will not only save you money, it will also create an asset for your homestead. For example, my father's South Carolina home is old enough that it predates current waste-disposal laws, and the wastewater from his sinks, tubs, showers, and washing machine is all piped into what greywater pro Art Ludwig calls a "drain out back" (a simple pipe running from the sink to the outside world). Since my father's climate is hot and dry and his soil is sandy and well-drained, he's able to plant blackberries, blueberries, and asparagus around the greywater effluent and boost production far beyond what he could expect from unwatered plants in his droughty climate.

If you live in a similarly arid location, especially one with relatively warm winters, you owe it to yourself to pick up a copy of Art Ludwig's excellent book *Create an Oasis with Greywater*. Ludwig walks you through building both simple and complex systems that can be used to put greywater to use, allowing you to eke out every drop of your water and to cut your water bill dramatically while keeping trees and shrubs happy.

Our original drain out back was a muddy mess.

Adding wood chips solved the problem and allowed us to grow King Stropharia mushrooms (which I'm irrigating in this photo). But the small harvest wasn't worth the extra effort.

While I loved Ludwig's book, though, it didn't suit our wet climate and cold winters. Due to our poorly drained clay soil and heavy rainfall, my husband and I are forced to mound up many parts of our garden so trees won't drown over the winter, and that's without adding any greywater to the system. Since we didn't have much incentive to collect our greywater, we initially sent our sink water to a drain out back. However, unlike on my father's homestead, our sink effluent resulted in a muddy mess outside the back door. Yuck! Adding wood chips beneath the drain slowed the slop factor (and produced a few edible mushrooms), but we never have enough wood chips to go around in the garden, let alone to "waste" an annual application for the sole purpose of soaking up our sink effluent. Was there a better solution to the greywater problem?

The first summer after planting, our greywater wetland was already doing its job well.

After reading Art Ludwig's book, I realized that a greywater wetland would be a great way to treat our household's dirty water while drying up our doorstep and creating a pretty patch of wildlife habitat in the process. In general, greywater wetlands are a good choice if you don't want to put any annual effort into the upkeep of your system, or if you live in an area like ours with lots and lots of rain. However, before I go any further, I should mention that greywater use in general is of dubious legality in many locations, so if you have building inspectors to please, everything in this section should be taken with a grain of salt. Another book by Ludwig, *Builder's Greywater Guide*, is available for those who want to stay on the up and up and jump through all the appropriate legal hoops.

Damselflies attracted by our greywater wetland soon got busy plucking mosquitoes and gnats out of the air.

Before you begin building a greywater wetland, you have several decisions to make, most of which pertain to your preferred level of complexity. Public water-treatment agencies are now using greywater wetlands to treat both storm water (runoff from pavement) and blackwater, and in these scenarios, it's worth putting in extra effort to make the bed of your wetland out of gravel, to include a drain pipe at the end, and to install baffles forcing the dirty water to move through as much medium as possible during its stay in the wetland. In many cases, these official treatment wetlands are also lined with plastic to prevent seepage of contaminated water into the ground.

However, the homesteader should keep in mind that each of these facets of a greywater wetland makes construction more time-consuming and expensive, and gravel and drains will also require periodic upkeep that you might not really be interested in performing. Since the average homesteader will simply be treating greywater from sinks, bathtubs, and laundry rooms, you might choose to follow my lead and keep your design as simple as possible. However, despite my urge for simplicity, please do make sure that your greywater wetland isn't located within one hundred feet of a well or natural body of water. This simple precaution will prevent your experiment from harming the surrounding environment and your own health.

In retrospect, raised walls around our wetland were more of a liability than an asset.

What makes up the simplest greywater-wetland design? All you really need is a pipe bringing water from the house, a slight indentation in the ground to contain the greywater, and some sort of cover over the effluent pipe so that vermin (and your pet dog) don't eat up scraps that float down from your dish-washing station. In terms of size, Ludwig recommends 100 to 400 square feet of wetland area for a four-person household, or about 1.5 to 3 square feet of wetland per gallon of greywater produced each day. Finally, you should aim for the width of your greywater wetland to be equal to about half of its length.

To be on the safe side, and to allow us to hook some of our gutters into the system, Mark and I created a wetland six feet by eleven feet with a slight gradient sloping downhill in the long direction. After a year and a half of use, I think that we probably overbuilt the system since we seldom see dampness over more than the first 24 square feet, but we also haven't hooked in all the gutters we plan to yet. Depending on your climate (wet or dry) and soil type (well-drained or moisture-retentive), you may want a larger or smaller wetland for your own trailerstead.

After planning the size of our wetland, we dug an indentation about eight inches deep, using the excess soil to mound up slight walls around the edges of the depression. In general, the indentation for a greywater wetland is meant to keep your dirty water from spilling out over the nearby lawn, but I probably overestimated our need for depth since water never pools in the wetland for more than a few minutes. Instead of containing water (since none needed to be contained) our wetland's walls ended up acting as a mowing barrier, which leads me to believe that we would have been better off applying that soil elsewhere, letting the wetland begin at ground level then dip down slightly below grade.

Although I'd originally envisioned our greywater wetland holding water that pooled at the surface, lack of standing water is actually a good thing since most health issues pertaining to greywater treatment occur when people come in contact with stagnant water that has been

Our radical plumbing job simply consisted of a pipe leading down from each sink basin, then a T sending the water downhill and into the wetland.

pooled long enough to allow disease bacteria to multiply. In contrast, soil microorganisms and simple filtration through the ground provide excellent treatment for all contaminants found in common household greywater, and also provide a physical barrier between problematic bacteria and their animal hosts. So your goal should be to ensure that your greywater sinks into the soil as quickly and as thoroughly as possible, which can be aided by a slight downhill tilt to spread the water across as large of an area of earth as possible.

Once you've dug out your wetland, the next step is to plumb a line from your sink (or other source of greywater) out to the wetland. If you're designing a more complex system, I once again refer you to *Create an Oasis with Greywater*, so here I'll just explain our very simple system. At the time this book is being written, we do our laundry using a wringer washer placed just above the wetland, and wash our bodies in a bathtub that leads to a separate area, so the only pipes entering our greywater wetland come from the kitchen sink. We chose to use what Ludwig calls "radical plumbing" to simplify the system as much as possible, letting water from each side of our sink flow down a separate 4-inch PVC pipe with no trap. Beneath our trailer, the pipes fit into the top of two separate

Water from some of our gutters flows into corrugated pipe that hooks into the back end of the T below our sink. The rainwater flushes out any buildup of food scraps in the line.

Ts, the downhill sides of which feed into another pair of 4-inch pipes that are buried just below grade, running at a 0.5 percent slope into the greywater wetland. The upper end of each T is a spot to attach piping from our gutters, which helps flush out any food scraps that begin to build up within our greywater-piping system. All of these pipes can be buried for convenience (making them easy to mow and walk across), but since water won't be standing within the pipes, there's no need to worry about digging a deep hole beneath the frost line.

Soon after the greywater wetland was built, it didn't look like much. But the wetland was already channeling mud away from our back door.

As a side note, I should mention that this type of radical plumbing *can* lead to a slight odor problem if you don't fit your pipes together perfectly, allowing anaerobic pools of water to collect at low points within the conduit. During our greywater wetland's first summer of operation, a slight swamp-gas odor began to waft up out of our sink for this reason, and being the busy homesteaders that we are, we addressed the problem . . . by keeping the strainers in the sink.

I was intrigued to realize that by the time we finally found a few hours to really fix the issue, nature had already solved it for us, eliminating the odor within a few weeks. I don't know if beneficial microorganisms colonized the pool of putrid water within our pipes or whether plant life took over similar pools outside, but within a month or so, the smell went away even when the strainers were removed, and we went back to calling our radical plumbing job a success. The moral of the story is, if that slight odor problem will bother you, or if you live in an area with lots of rats and other vermin that might crawl up your drainpipe and into your home, you'll want to install a trap.

Rocks around the inlet keep dogs from gobbling up food scraps.

So now you have a pipe running from your kitchen sink to a little hole in the earth. Are you done? Not yet. The one bit of complexity that I feel is worth your time is to make the area where greywater runs into your wetland critter-proof. Ludwig suggests several options in his book (some of which require regular maintenance), but I opted for the free-and-easy method of piling rocks all around the inlet. I used some old bricks we had lying around to create a solid surface for the greywater to spill out onto, which will prevent erosion when water gushes out of the pipes, then I dry-laid rock walls and a top over an area about three feet long. I was pleased to find that, even though our dog likes to dig up huge areas of the garden in search of rodents and will break into a chicken pasture to eat up kitchen scraps, our rocked inlet hasn't seen a single incursion in all the time that our greywater wetland has been in place.

Cattails are a good species to include in greywater wetlands since the hardy plants thrive in high-nutrient environments.

If you wanted, you could stop there and your greywater wetland would work just fine. However, I love wetland plants, and I wanted my wetland to green up fast, so I dug about half a dozen cattails out of a nearby swamp and installed them in our muddy indentation. The cattails soon sent up shoots and began to grow, and they've now completely covered the area that stays permanently damp. You could add other wetland plants as well, with horsetails, sedges, water plantain, and sweet flags being other top choices in our region. But cattails alone seem to be doing the job admirably in our wetland, while bringing beauty to what used to be a mud hole outside our back door. Plus, the cattails turn our wetland into a possible source of food, so maybe our greywater-treatment system is an edible planting after all.

We simplified piping to our greywater wetland by doing laundry just above the wetland entrance. Although a wringer washer has no energy benefits over a modern washing machine, these old-timey washers drain completely, so they can be left outside during the winter, saving space in our trailer for more essential appliances. Wringer washers are also simple enough that the average homesteader can make repairs rather than hiring a specialist.

I'll end this section with a few simple admonitions to ensure you get the most out of your greywater wetland. Although you definitely shouldn't pour chemicals down your drain once you install a greywater wetland, some less-than-savory compounds are likely to end up in your treatment area anyway. However, as long as you choose the less-harmful cleaning agents and use them in small doses, chances are your wetland will still thrive.

We regularly release unscented (but not particularly natural) dish detergent, a little bit of bleach and toothpaste and mouthwash, plus some powdered laundry detergent into our wetland, and the cattails lap it right up. Some of these chemicals are on Ludwig's no-no list (although he agrees that they don't cause many problems at low doses). Common household chemicals that you should absolutely avoid sending down the drain once you install your wetland include drain cleaners (use a snake instead), porcelain cleaners (use boiling water and elbow grease instead), and borax. Other no-nos that aren't quite so terrible include chlorine bleach and non-chlorine bleach containing sodium perborate; detergents that whiten, soften, or contain enzymes; and powdered laundry detergents containing sodium fillers. (Liquid laundry detergents are better for the health of your wetland.)

Despite the small lifestyle changes you may need to make in order to keep your greywater wetland happy, chances are you'll find it to be a no-work, cost-cutting measure that easily fits into your permaculture homestead after the initial installation. During our own wetland's second year of operation, I was interested to notice that the greywater-treatment system was one of the few aspects of our homestead that simply did its job with no required upkeep on our part. In fact, the only time I spent with our wetland this past summer involved watching dragonflies perch on nearby plants and enjoying the show as our cattails burst into bloom. Like the next project in this chapter, the only change I would have made to our greywater system would have been to build our wetland several years sooner in order to give us the pleasure of additional years of wildlife watching right outside our back door.

Experiments with humanure

Our composting-toilet system combines features of outhouses with the hot-composting method outlined in *The Humanure Handbook*.

As I explained in the last section, our greywater is channeled into a wetland for treatment, which begs the question: what do we do with our blackwater (human wastes)? The traditional solution—a septic system—was vastly out of our price range when we first moved to the farm, and my research also suggested that those mainstream systems weren't really very environmentally friendly in the first place. Instead, Mark and I opted to build a composting toilet in order to turn human waste into garden fertilizer, all at a very low cost.

Our composting-toilet system is loosely based on John Jenkins's *The Humanure Handbook*, which you can read online for free at humanurehandbook.com/contents.html. When I was in the researching stage of our own project, I vastly appreciated Jenkins's advice on building and managing a hot-composting system that kills disease-causing microorganisms, but neither Mark nor I was in love with the idea of pooping into a bucket and then carrying the slop outdoors to a compost bin at regular intervals. (Actually, Mark's reaction was much stronger than that, and may have involved swearing. "#*!% no!" he told me.) So, instead of following Jenkins's plans to the letter, we decided to build an outdoor structure that composted waste on site, combining the most sanitary features of both an outhouse and a composting toilet.

Our completed composting toilet is screened off from view on the back and on the most-visible side. This photo was taken soon after initial construction, when fresh sawdust was being stored in two bins for later use.

We planned our composting toilet to have three bins at the bottom, a platform for people to walk and sit on over top, and a raised roof yet higher up. The two bins on either side would be filled with human waste during alternating years, allowing a solid twelve months of composting action between deposit and garden application. In the meantime, the middle bin would store sawdust or other carbonaceous materials, a scoop of which would be tossed down the hole after each use to prevent our waste from attracting flies and other vermin.

We soon moved the sawdust out of the bins and into a trash can.

After two years of use, we're quite happy with our composting toilet and would do only a few things differently. First, the spaces we left for aeration purposes between the bins' slats weren't necessary and instead allowed critters to creep inside and then drag used toilet paper out into the woods. (Ugh! Time for Mark to say "I told you so.") To fix that problem, we ended up filling in all of the gaps, and I definitely recommend that those following our lead build solid, rather than slatted, walls around each bin.

Second, storing sawdust within the central bin was subpar, since those aforementioned critters dragged used toilet paper into the supposedly clean sawdust. We ended up moving the extra carbonaceous material into a closed trash can, and we now scoop out a two-gallon bucketful at intervals to keep beside the seat for daily use.

The first year's humanure was much appreciated by our dwarf apple trees.

Finally, after removing the first year's compost to apply to our dwarf apple trees, we felt like the bin's contents were too dry and could have benefited from frequent waterings. In the near future, we hope to install a gutter-and-rain-barrel system attached to the composting toilet's roof to make it easy to add moisture to active bins. While we're at it, we'll also install a hand-washing station to promote proper hygiene without tracking our muddy boots back through the house on days when we're working outside.

Those few caveats aside, my reluctant husband was soon won over by our composting-toilet system. Although he adamantly opposed the initial construction, Mark recently reported with glee that he'd watched a hawk swoop down to capture a wren while taking care of his morning business. "That's one of my most inspiring bird sightings since we moved to the farm!" he exclaimed. You definitely can't get *that* kind of experience while sitting on the pot inside a modern house!

Case study: Early retirement in a trailer

Harry and Zoe's double-wide has become the center of a beautiful homestead.

Photo credit: Harry and Zoe

When Harry bought his 1984-model double-wide in 1999, the structure was already atop a permanent foundation on a small rural acreage. Harry was delighted to find an affordable, secluded place to live, and wasn't concerned that mobile homes tend to depreciate in value. His goal was to work toward an early retirement, becoming a full-time homesteader in the process.

"We do this because we love it," Harry explained.

Photo credit: Harry and Zoe

Along the way, Harry picked up a mate, who is also enthusiastic about living the simple life. When asked how Zoe felt about his choice of a mobile home, Harry noted that his spouse "affirmed the decision" by moving in soon after they met in 2002. Both Zoe and Harry "value self-sufficiency and a rural lifestyle. Our hobby farm is our retirement dream and it is a conscious choice," Harry explained. "We do this because we love it."

Photo credit: Harry and Zoe

Harry and Zoe's garden is full of homemade improvements, like rebar tomato cages (right side of the photo), a greenhouse (currently covered with shade cloth in this picture), a shade-house frame (on the left side of the photo, currently uncovered), and various outbuildings.

The homestead that sprang up around Harry and Zoe's trailer is both beautiful and functional. Their extensive garden provides tomatoes, cucumbers, squash, lettuce, spinach, onions, garlic, basil, cilantro, rosemary, marjoram, thyme, lavender, and plenty of fresh flowers, along with berries, melons, grapes, temperate tree fruit, and lemons. Zoe cultivates the dwarf lemon trees in pots, moving them inside to a south-facing window in their trailer for the winter.

A shade house allows Harry and Zoe to eat lettuce and spinach during July even though they garden in hot-summered zone 6, and they also grow greens right through the winter in their small greenhouse. The homesteaders use a heated stock tank full of aquatic plants to help stabilize the temperature in the greenhouse year-round, and a thermostat-controlled electric heater keeps the air above freezing during cold winter nights.

I could fully imagine Mark and me becoming Zoe and Harry in another couple of decades, partly because I would like to aspire to such a

Harry built a boot brush from a poly push broom that he cut in half and fastened to two pieces of landscape timber with wood screws. The timbers are anchored into the soil using rebar pegs driven into holes in the timbers. Repeating the project with a discarded broom and scrap lumber would make the boot cleaner cost next to nothing, while helping prevent tracking the garden into your home.

Photo credit: Harry and Zoe

well-kept-up homestead, but also because of the duo's focus on partnership. When I originally wrote about one of Harry's projects, he gently admonished me, noting that "Harry and Zoe are an equal partnership—we work as a team to plan and carry out projects. Often, one of us devotes more time or effort to a project, but the goal is always to improve our standard of living."

Harry tends to take the lead in projects that make use of his building skills, like the window awnings profiled in an earlier chapter and the homemade boot brush and mud grate shown above. Meanwhile, Zoe spearheads projects that require a green thumb, keeping the garden vibrantly alive and productive. "The most common failure in homesteader relationships is obvious," Harry noted. "One partner is far more invested in homesteading than the other." He and his wife's equal partnership keep

The couple's second line of defense against tracked-in mud is a grate on the porch that operates like a mat, but that allows grime to fall through to the ground below. Bar grates like the one Harry installed can often be found in scrapyards and are also available from steel service centers.

Photo credit: Harry and Zoe

the homestead humming along efficiently, and their shared labor turns work into play.

What further advice does the duo have to share with homesteaders who are at an earlier stage of their farm-building adventure? Harry and Zoe heartily recommend that you think long and hard about whether trailersteading is really your cup of tea since "you will most likely find it difficult or impossible to sell your trailer." And even before would-be homesteaders move onto an acreage, Harry suggests familiarizing yourself with the Agricultural Extension Service. "The Extension Services offer all of their information for free online," Harry explained. "The most important reason to use Extension information is to avoid repeating other people's mistakes." I heartily second Harry's recommendation, with the additional tip that in-person classes are often available as well, some of which allow homesteaders to bring home free honeybees or hand-grafted apple trees for as little as $1 apiece.

I like to end all of my interviews by asking the trailersteaders whether they'd accept a large, modern home if it came free of charge, but with the usual upkeep and tax burden. "No way!" Harry responded. "First, we would not want to live in close proximity to neighbors. Second, even if it was on a secluded, rural acreage, we would not want to pay the additional taxes and utility costs. We would not trade our home for anyone else's!" Zoe agreed. "Been there, done that," she said, "and I like this a whole lot better."

Outdoor living rooms

Happy trailersteaders often move much of their living outside during warm weather.

While water and waste management around your trailer can improve your standard of living, you'll probably receive the most day-to-day satisfaction from the addition of porches, which can become primary outdoor living spaces whenever weather permits. At first, I thought there wasn't much to say about outdoor living areas beyond "build a porch and enjoy it," but the more I paid attention to the way we manage our outdoor spaces, the more I realized that the topic could fill a book all by itself. Human beings love comfort, and there's a reason why so many of us spend nearly every day inside—the outdoors can be hot, cold, windy, wet, buggy, and generally unpleasant to be around. So the trick to creating outdoor living areas that you'll use is to work around the wild, ensuring that your family enjoys the benefits of outdoor living without having to deal with the truly negative aspects of the outdoors.

During the growing season, our porches are filled with curing sunflower-seed heads, onions, garlic, butternut squash, and much more.

Excessive summer heat is one of the biggest reasons that people steer clear of their porches and huddle around the air conditioner instead. Dealing with this issue is similar to understanding passive-solar methods of managing the temperature within your trailer, which I explained in more depth in a previous chapter. After a year of meals enjoyed on our south-facing porch, we realized that the biggest impediment to utilizing the space was blazing sunlight shining in through the open west side to cook us in the afternoon and evening, so we used sheets of plastic-lattice material and fast-growing scarlet runner beans to provide cooling shade along with a bit of beauty. Similarly, we moved our freezer and summer kitchen to the north-facing porch to prevent the sun from roasting areas that we needed to stay cool, and we used insulation beneath the metal on one of our porches to further circumvent the sun's rays.

If bugs, rather than heat, are the bane of your existence, you may choose to screen in your porch, and you may also need to create a solid wall on one side if strong winds frequently blow rain inside. Maybe you'll want to add a ceiling fan or a light for evening dining, a rocket stove for off-grid cooking, or a sink for easy garden-vegetable preparation in the open air. Like Mark, you may want a workbench for inventing, or a designated spot on the porch to stack split firewood during the winter for easy access. On the other hand, maybe you don't want a porch at all, just a patio with stones to keep the mud down and a grill for outdoor cooking. Plant some flowers to brighten your day and pay attention to your local conditions, and soon you too will be dining, bathing, relaxing, cooking, curing vegetables, processing seeds, drying food, and inventing in the great outdoors.

Outbuildings

Beyond taking full advantage of outdoor living spaces, the other trait that most trailersteads have in common is the copious use of outbuildings. On our own farm, we enjoy a large barn, two chicken coops, a goat shed, a composting toilet, and a woodshed in addition to our trailer, and other profiled trailersteaders have also built or bought similar structures. Wendy and Mikey (profiled in the section "Cheap and green") used shipping containers to expand their workshop into the outdoors, while David and Mary (profiled in the section "An incognito trailer") created their structures using satellite dishes and surplus materials. To jump-start your own imagination, here are two of David's unique outbuildings to consider.

David and Mary built their new woodshed primarily using free materials.

David and Mary's newest outbuilding is a woodshed that the couple built for next to nothing. David brought the steel studs home for free from the plant where he used to work, he found surplus fiberglass panels for the floor at a significant discount, and he created a roof out of rubber sheets that were being discarded from gas-well water-storage tanks. The wire that prevents stacked wood from falling out the sides was left over from another project, and, in the end, the couple only had to buy the four-by-four posts and screws at full price.

David and Mary's satellite-dish gazebo serves double duty as a moist spot for mushroom logs and as a cool place for the couple to relax during hot summer afternoons.

Photo credit: David and Mary

Even more ingenious is David's use of a large, aluminum-mesh satellite dish to create a shade-house gazebo for his mushroom logs. The satellite dish is supported by four-by-four posts, around which plastic-lattice material was wrapped to provide a support for ivy that will further cool and shade the interior. David noted that the sprinkler head shown in the second photo was eventually replaced by individual spray misters, which seemed to work better at keeping the mushroom logs moist. In addition, David planted some grapevines around the structure initially, but the wet, shady conditions promoted fungal diseases, so the grapes were ripped out and replaced with hardy kiwis. Soon the gazebo will serve yet a third function—as a trellis for an edible vine!

While the type of outbuildings you eventually build will inevitably be very specific to your farm and needs, I do have a few tips for managing trailersteading sprawl. First, consider the sun when selecting your outbuildings' locations—woodsheds will dry your firewood much more quickly if placed in direct sunlight, while shade houses and root cellars are better located on the north side of your trailer or in the shadow of trees or of a hillside.

Next, think about access. Permaculturalists talk about zones radiating out from your home, with the closer locations being reserved for portions of the homestead that require daily attention. Using this logic, you'll want to place frequently used outbuildings a little closer to your trailer, while those with the potential to smell (like composting toilets) or to eat your garden (like goats) should be located a bit farther away.

Finally, don't forget to scrounge around for free and cheap materials. Chances are you can build elegant outbuildings for a song just like David and Mary did!

Case study: A holler full of family
Scarberry Holler

Alice and Jimmy's trailer (foreground) is so close to Kayla's house ...

...that mother and daughter can communicate using a margarine tub on a string.

Jimmy and Alice Scarberry moved into their trailer in 1978 when they were just beginning to create their own family. Nearly four decades later, their younger daughter Kayla and Kayla's husband Andy live so close by that mother and daughter can pass messages between the two houses in an old margarine tub hooked up to a line and pulley.

"Jimmy's father and mother used to live in what is now Kayla's house when we first moved here," Alice explained. "And Kayla loved to look in a tub just like that one for notes and candy from her Papaw. Now Kayla and her nephew play the same game when Jedd comes to visit."

The Scarberrys bought their home for $15,000 in 1978, a figure that included half an acre of land.

Photo credit: Jimmy and Alice Scarberry

After sinking about $7,000 into renovations over the years, their trailer is now so well disguised that a tax assessor recently mistook the residence for a modular home. Their insurance company currently values the home at $96,000, a 75% increase in value (after factoring in inflation).

Family ties in Scarberry Holler aren't limited to a simple message system. In fact, back before city water reached this rural valley, seven related households all shared a single spring. "If you wanted to take a shower," Kayla explained, "you'd need to phone the families up the holler to make sure they weren't using water too." Alice added, "When we got city water, Kayla was afraid to step under the shower head—the water pressure was so strong, she thought it would knock her down."

Despite having to schedule bathing times, the Scarberrys enjoyed (and still enjoy) living in such close proximity to their kin. Recently, Jimmy, Alice, Kayla, and Andy were stringing beans together on the parents' back deck when they heard laughter drifting down from up on the hill. The four soon realized that Jimmy's sister's family was preparing green beans on their porch at the same time, and Kayla was disappointed to realize that her cousins were having more fun than her immediate family was. "So we decided to pretend we were having a ball too," Kayla explained. "And before we knew it, we were having so much fun stringing those beans, our cousins were jealous of *us*."

Turning a trailer into a home

The original trailer contains the current kitchen, dining room, and work room, while the bedrooms, bathroom, and living room are found in the addition. Both parts of the house have been flawlessly renovated to form a cohesive whole.

Every residence on Scarberry Holler isn't a trailer, but Jimmy's and Alice's home is . . . not that you would realize their house's humble pedigree from walking by the outside or through the inside. When the couple moved in, the original 600-square-foot trailer from the 1960s had already been expanded into a 1,480-square-foot hybrid home using additions on the south and east sides. "We moved here from a 10-by-50-foot trailer in a trailer park in the city," Alice remembered. "When we settled into our new home, I was over the moon to have so much room. I had closets!"

Alice's simple but elegant design sense is evident in Kayla's old bedroom, which has become a guest room now that Kayla lives in her own house next door.

Since then, the family has slowly remodeled both the trailer and the add-on portions until their home has become an elegant and functional living space. The Scarberries ripped out the carpet and installed laminate flooring, they painted the wall paneling, and they changed out the kitchen cabinets. In the energy department, they slowly worked their way through an oil stove, a coal stove, a wood stove, and electric baseboard heaters before settling on a heat pump as the cheapest and easiest solution. Trailer windows were replaced with more modern apertures and exterior Masonite siding was replaced with vinyl siding.

Although the family spent about $7,000 on major renovations over the years, Alice was quick to mention that most of the furnishings were yard-sale finds or hand-me-downs. The result is a home so beautiful that a tax assessor recently mistook the trailer for a modular home. Only after Jimmy explained that his family lives in a trailer did taxes return to manageable levels.

A deck and porch provide extra room for working and relaxing.

Outside, a wooden deck on the south side of the house and a covered porch on the north side provide plenty of room for relaxation and bean snapping. The Scarberrys made the floor for their porch out of flagstones cemented into place, which cost almost nothing, and which stays cool in the summer (although the surface does become slippery during storms). A screened-in section of the porch has served as a chicken hospital, a tomato-ripening station, a spot for storing garbage away from animals, and as a bug-free room in which their grandchildren can play.

Raising an avid homesteader

Kayla nursed this hen back to health after the bird's back was torn apart by an aggressive rooster. Now Child (named by Kayla's young nephew) enjoys her own tractor.

Alice and Jimmy grew up canning and gardening because that's what rural people do in southwest Virginia, but their daughter Kayla has become enthusiastic about more modern methods of homesteading in addition to the old ways. As a result, Kayla is glad to have her parents next door not just for sharing time, but also for sharing space—when she runs out of room for planting fruit trees in her own yard, Kayla's orchard can spill over into her parents' lawn. And the chicken tractors that her father and husband built can be dragged not just across Kayla's own lawn, but onto her parents' grass and even into the neighbors' yard beyond. In fact, I even glimpsed garlic hung up to cure in the rafters of a picnic shelter at the upper edge of Kayla's parents' property, a sure sign that Kayla had decided to put that relaxation spot to more productive use as well.

On the east end of her parents' trailer, a small pantry accessible only from the outdoors showcases the overlap between mother's and daughter's passions. Alice and Kayla have lined the shelves with preserved bounty from their gardens, much of which they packed into cans at a local cannery. "Mom cut up onions and vegetables for a full day in preparation," Kayla explained. "Then we went together to cook up vegetable soup in the cannery's big pots. We ended up with over ten gallons of soup, plus another four gallons of stock after running out of some of the vegetables." Along with jams, corn, and pickles processed at home, every pantry shelf was already full when I visited in August.

The pantry added onto the east side of the trailer is full of preserved food that Kayla and Alice grew and canned together.

A gift from her parents, this bench makes an elegant addition to Kayla's front porch.

Mother and daughter also share an interest in crafting. After seeing a wooden bench made out of an old bed frame that was being sold for $150, Alice decided to try her hand at a DIY version. She and her husband quickly converted a $10 yard-sale find into her own bench, with the bed's headboard forming the bench's back and with the footboard cut in half to make the sides. Kayla used similar logic to re-create silverware wind chimes that she added to her mother's porch collection and that she also sells in her Etsy shop (www.etsy.com/shop/buffalogalcountry).

Saving time for family

Living in a trailer allows Alice to focus on the things that give her joy, like her family and her collection of wind chimes.

When asked about the biggest advantage of trailer life, Alice mentioned ease of upkeep, but also emphasized the affordability factor. In 1977, $15,000 was sufficient to purchase the family's home along with half an acre of land, and that reasonable price tag has allowed the couple to focus on their family ever since.

Their fixation has paid off by producing a mother-daughter bond that would make most of us jealous. While their husbands are away at work, the two women regularly eat breakfast and share chores together, so it's no surprise that Alice missed her daughter when Kayla and Andy were gone camping for a weekend this past summer. In fact, the two generations work and play so well together that the younger couple opted to take Kayla's parents along when they went out of town for their third honeymoon a few weeks later.

Living in a trailer obviously won't ensure that your family is as close knit as the Scarberrys, but keeping costs low so you can spend time doing what really matters is at the root of voluntary simplicity. Alice's one piece of advice for wannabe trailersteaders mirrors that theme. "Be sure to buy a home large enough to allow your family to grow," Alice recommends. It never hurts to make it easy for your adult daughter to move in next door either.

Lessons learned on the trailerstead

Starting a trailerstead from scratch is an exercise in patience. When my husband-to-be and I moved to our farm in September 2006, our free trailer had big holes in the walls instead of windows and the forty-year-old structure had been deemed uninhabitable by its previous owner. Meanwhile, what was to become our garden looked more like a briar patch, with thorny branches that reached up over my shoulders and caught in my hair as I tried to walk past. But as the years progressed, Mark and I slowly tamed the wilds and turned our farm into a peaceable kingdom. I hope you'll be inspired by these final images, documenting the growth of our trailerstead from a single-wide amid the weeds to the paradise we live in today.

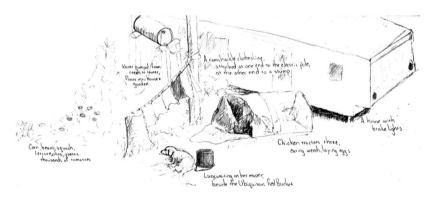

In 2007, our homestead was very simple. We carried jugs of drinking water to our trailer from a neighbor's spring and washed with water pumped to a raised 55-gallon tank, then carried indoors in a red plastic bucket.

As you can see, our farm had very humble beginnings, which taught us our first trailersteading lesson: starting out with nearly nothing means that every little improvement to our standard of living is a pure delight. If we'd been lucky enough to move into a homestead with all of the amenities we enjoy today, would we truly relish the wonder of running water on demand? Similarly, if we were able to jump ahead to the fully established homestead that I dream of one day creating, with apple and pear fruits dripping from the trees that are currently whippersnappers in our yard, would the harvest still taste as good without the memories of nurturing our growing orchard for a dozen years in between planting and harvest?

Over time, our homestead slowly emerged from the weeds. By 2008, we had built a very ramshackle awning on the front of our trailer and were beginning to establish our gardens.

Three years later, our wood-stove alcove and eight-by-twenty addition had expanded our living quarters and improved our ability to provide winter heat.

Meanwhile, I wonder how many skills and experiences we would have missed out on had a fully evolved homestead fallen into our laps rather than having to be built piece by piece as funds and energy allowed. Would Mark and I enjoy our current strong relationship if we hadn't been forced to learn how to build an eight-by-twenty-foot extension together on a shoestring budget? While struggling with two-by-fours, the project seemed to stress our emerging bond, but now I

In 2012, our microbusiness selling chicken waterers over the Internet took off, freeing up cash to pay a friendly neighbor to improve our buildings. We soon had a new woodshed, a couple of porches, a solid roof on the barn, and (not too long after this photo was taken), a third porch and a composting toilet. The blue tarp is shielding our previous solution to the excrement problem—a hole in the ground covered by an adult-sized potty chair. Who has time to keep outhouse facilities out of the rain when you're busy growing all the vegetables you can eat?

In this final photo, dating from July 2014, you can see that our homestead continues to shape up. The big poles in the foreground are a support structure for our high-density apple planting, one of many garden experiments that fill our time now that our basic infrastructure is largely in place.

find that the relationship we forged in the heat of adversity continues to stand up to the test of time.

As a bonus, choosing to sink our savings into land instead of into a fancy house means that everything we see in every direction now belongs to us, with no debt hanging over our heads. We have the freedom to embark on crazy experiments that our neighbors neither know nor care about, and we have the privilege of eschewing off-farm work, simply improving our homestead when extra funds allow. So if, as one of our critics proposed, this makes us uncivilized, lazy, and irresponsible, then I'm all for laziness!

In fact, I heartily recommend that you join the ranks of the uncivilized. By working smart rather than hard and by starting with a home that truly fits within your budget, you too can see all of the benefits of an emerging trailerstead as it brings each of your dreams to life. Follow your bliss and you'll be halfway there!

Acknowledgments

Like all of my books, this title grew out of conversations with readers of our blog and with family and friends. I'm especially indebted to the trailer-dwellers who opened their lives to my nosy questions, and to Bradley who didn't mind me hanging over his shoulder with a camera all summer long. Longtime blog-reader Roland and world's-greatest-mother Adrianne were invaluable in the initial editing stages, while the folks at Skyhorse turned my buggy manuscript into a polished paperback. My husband came up with the idea of living in a trailer and also taught me that living simply is not only ethically sound, it's also a fun and inspiring adventure. Last, but certainly not least, I'm eternally grateful to kind readers who leave reviews on retailer websites, tell their friends about my books, and share their enthusiasm—you are why I write.

About the author

Anna Hess dreamed about moving back to the land ever since her parents dragged her off their family farm at the age of eight. She worked as a field biologist and nonprofit organizer before acquiring fifty-eight acres and a husband, then quit her job to homestead full time. She admits that real farm life involves a lot more hard work than her childhood memories entailed, but the reality is much more fulfilling and she loves pigging out on sun-warmed strawberries and experimenting with no-till gardening, mushroom propagation, and chicken pasturing.

She also enjoys writing about her adventures, both on her blog at WaldenEffect.org, and in her books. Her first paperback, *The Weekend Homesteader*, helped thousands of homesteaders-to-be find ways to fit their dreams into the hours left over from a full-time job, while *The Naturally Bug-Free Garden* offered up tips for working with nature to keep insect damage in an organic garden to a minimum. In addition, a heaping handful of ebooks help homesteaders work chickens, cover crops, storage vegetables, and more into a permaculture homestead.

Index